AMEN
MINISTRIES
Founder of
Sunshine Div.

A STRONG GRIP

The Stories of Oregon's
BUD LEWIS
An Ageless Icon

Sheri Clostermann Anderson

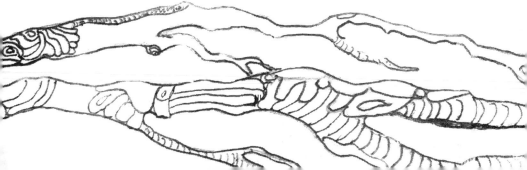

A Strong Grip:
The Stories of Oregon's Bud Lewis, An Ageless Icon

Copyright 2017 © Sheri Clostermann Anderson
ISBN 978-0-9993313-0-9

Publisher
Leo's Rose City Press
Portland, Oregon 97221
leosrosecitypress.com

Cover Art © Diane Lewis and Sherry Wachter
Book design by Sherry Wachter

Note to the reader: *References in this book to specific people, places, organizations and events are based on personal views and recollections. Details related to WWII campaigns and battles vary depending on sources. In all cases, attempts have been made to provide context and to be as accurate as possible.*

1 2 3 4 5 6 7 8 9 10

Contents

THE STRENGTH OF THE GIANT SEQUOIA
(SEQUOIADENDRON GIGANTEUM)

It is Earth's largest tree and largest living thing by volume. With a lifespan of up to 3,000 years, its genus dates back 200 million years to when dinosaurs roamed the earth.

The secret to the Giant Sequoia's longevity and capacity to thrive may be in its ability to adapt to its environment. Its roots spread and intertwine with vegetation over more than an acre.

The Sequoia's bark can be up to three feet thick yet Native Americans found its peelings strong and pliable enough to use for clothing.

"I've got to show you a tree," Bud said after we discussed the idea of compiling his memoirs. "It's magnificent. I'll bet it's 150 years old! It has grown over and around a curb but not into the street. You have to see it."

If there is one thing about Bud Lewis, and there are many, it is the example he sets for those around him. His stories reveal a life well and exuberantly lived. The tree that has captured him grows on a quiet neighborhood street in Portland's Southwest hills. It towers over everything around it and can be seen for miles. Its roots, some of which are apparent near the surface of the ground, extend in all directions. The trunk is oblong – an accommodation to the curb and the street that undoubtedly came in long after the roots had been established.

The tree is an icon to the neighborhood, an engagement with the life around it.

—SCA

BUD (CENTER IN KNICKERS) AT AGE 7, WITH
YOUNGER SISTER BOBBIE, OLDER BROTHER BILL
AND YOUNGER BROTHER JACK.

Chapter 1

STARTING NORTH OF THE BORDER

Deep in the prairie lands of Central Canada some 70 miles north of Calgary in the province of Alberta is, or was, Mayton. Best described as a hamlet, it was there Aug. 8, 1920, the day Leland Stanford Lewis, now better known as "Bud," was born. (He's named after an uncle, not the founder of Stanford University, although he says allusions to the University's fame have been useful.)

Mayton once boasted an abundance of cows and a resulting creamery. Continued fortune was banked on a train eventually coming through. That it never did sent the town sliding toward its demise.

In the early 1900s, when times were tough everywhere, Bud's grandparents on both sides moved up to Canada from the U.S. to find work. His parents eventually met in the Alberta town of Innisfail. They married there and set out to live off the land as farmers. "It's what you did when you didn't know what else to do," Bud says, adding that his dad was no farmer. In retrospect, he allows that his mother was not either.

When little Leland, already known as Bud, was three years old, one of the family fields caught fire. Taking it as a sign that it was time to leave both the farming life and Canada, his parents packed up Bud, older brother Bill and younger sister Bobbie and headed south toward California. By Portland, their money ran out and staying seemed the best option. Bud's father found a job first as a cement worker and then with the U.S. Postal Service. That steady income allowed the Lewis family to buy a home and settle in for good.

AT AGE 10, PERFORMING A STUNT THAT WOULD COME IN HANDY LATER IN LIFE.

As to his early years, Bud says he was a normal if somewhat mischievous kid playing around with his siblings in ways that frequently caught his father's attention and the occasional disciplinary strap. "I wasn't bad, just typical," he says. Until, of course, that day at about age 10, when Bud and two cohorts entered a brief and memorable foray into the world of crime. The scene was Fairley's Drugstore, Northeast 72nd and Sandy Blvd. The crime was gum thievery. As to whether it was premeditated, Bud admits it probably was. "We were in the drugstore and we weren't there to say hello to Mr. Fairley."

Watchful to young boys and their antics, Mr. Fairley caught the young thieves gum-handed before they could make their getaway. With great chagrin, Bud now confesses that it was a terrible thing for them to do. "All the things I had been taught," he laments. "And there I was stealing something!"

Fairley, Bud remembers, played the boys like a fine violin. "He told us he was thinking of calling a patrol car to take us to the police station. That nearly scared us to death!" Probably seeing the lack of evil intent in the boys' hearts, Fairley did not turn them in, nor did he make good on his threat to call their fathers. What he did was gain sniffling promises from the terrified trio that they would never steal again. "We promised," Bud says. "And we really meant it."

Years later when he was a patrolman, Bud stopped in at that long-ago crime scene and thanked druggist Fairley for catching him and his friends and preventing their descent toward delinquency. "I told him it was the best thing in the world for the good of three young boys. He scared the wits out of us!"

High school for Bud was Benson, a trade-oriented school for boys. "Apparently, my parents thought it was best for me to learn a skill. They definitely did not want me to be a farmer!"

Bud also spent time there developing the athletic abilities that would prove valuable as the years progressed. He made the varsity baseball

A MISCHIEVOUS-LOOKING BUD AT ABOUT THE AGE HE AND BUDDIES CONDUCTED THEIR GUM-HEIST AT THE LOCAL PHARMACY.

team, and played some football. That sport, however, proved too expensive to pursue. A tooth kept getting knocked out, and since he had to pay for the dental work himself, he decided the pain was not worth the gain so he chose not to continue.

A good alternative and a worthwhile pastime was joining the Oregon National Guard.

POSING IN A FAVORITE OUTFIT.

CHAPTER 2

HEEDING THE CALL

At Benson High School in the fall of 1936, Bud was already 6 feet 3½ inches, a sophomore and too young to join the Oregon National Guard. He was one of many too-young-to-joins who were inspired by the achievements of Jesse Owens, Louis Zamperini, the boys in the University of Washington boat, and other Americans who bested Adolf Hitler's youth at the summer's Olympics in Berlin. Patriotism was high.

Higher still, for Bud, was the lure of military pay.

"I told them I was 18," he says when he went in to sign up for the 41st Division, the same one his father had been in. "But they knew. The recruiting officer looked me right in the eye and told me I was born in 1918. 'OK,' I said, and was in." As far as the U.S. military was concerned, Bud's age defied his birth certificate until his discharge from active service in 1945. His and a lot of others.

At first, military service was Tuesday evening drills at the Portland Armory on N.W. 10th and Couch. The pay was $1 a drill.

Being in the Service Company of the 186th Infantry Regiment, 41st Division, meant drilling in first aid, map reading, truck driving and other jobs necessary to support an infantry regiment. "We also dealt with weapons, and vehicles," he says.

THE PROUD MEMBERS OF THE NATIONAL GUARD BASKETBALL TEAM.
PORTLAND'S NORTONIA HOTEL SPONSORED THE TEAM.

Bud's specific job was to be a truck driver and command the vehicle that held the company kitchen. Making sure the food got to those it was intended to feed was an important job, definitely key to their overall success.

Key, too, was his participation on two basketball teams. It was the era of the new two-handed set shot and Bud was particularly adept at it. "I generally played forward but sometimes center," he says. With essentially the same players, he proudly remembers that both teams were quite good.

In summers, the Service Company had two-week training camps at Fort Lewis and Camp Murray in Washington and at Camp Clatsop in Oregon. There, with bolt-action rifles, they learned and perfected their marksmanship skills and expanded their abilities as soldiers.

On Sept. 16, 1940, the Burke-Wadsworth Act, also known as the Selective Training & Service Act of 1940, was passed into law enabling the first peacetime conscription in U.S. history. All men between the ages of 21 and 35 were required to register for potential military service. A lottery selected those who went into immediate service for one year. By the law's expiration in 1947, some 10 million men had been inducted into military service.

Although technically not yet 21, military calculations had Bud sufficiently old enough for a year of immediate and active service. His Guard unit, considered one of the best in the country because of their extensive training on those Tuesday nights and summer weeks, was mobilized the very day the Selective Service Act passed. They became part of the 41st Division that included soldiers from Oregon, Washington, Idaho, Montana and Wyoming. With their shoulder sleeve insignia of a setting sun, they were nicknamed the "Sunset Division." The designation gained further significance on Jan. 17, 1946, when Oregon's Highway 26 that extends from Portland to the setting sun at Cannon Beach was renamed the Sunset Highway and dedicated to the men of the 41st.

Training took place at Fort Lewis and prepared the men for whatever might arise during their presumed one-year of service. Instruction for their individual jobs took much of the days, as did physical fitness activities – running, climbing, lifting, crawling – culminating in trials on the obstacle course to test conditioning and endurance. When their course tests came, Bud tied for first place both times they were conducted. (Thirteen years later he again took first place when, as a training captain, he competed against his enlisted men.)

Also helping soldiers get and keep in shape was boxing. "I wasn't really a boxer but I thought it was an interesting sport," Bud says, remembering being challenged to a match one day by a rough, tough-appearing soldier. "I agreed to it, and by the time we started a few men had gathered around to watch."

As the match continued, Bud became apprehensive. "I stung this guy a few times when we started off, I don't remember if it was with my right or my left. Well, he got mad, really mad and looked like he wanted to kill me! He came back with big, roundhouse swings, not ones you'd throw at a friendly exercise match.

"Then he threw a wild swing and missed. And that made him even angrier!" What followed was Bud getting him with an uppercut. "My glove didn't go more than 12 or 15 inches, but it knocked him out! His eyes rolled back and he fell flat, like a tree. I thought I'd killed him! He came around a few seconds later, but stayed away from me after that." From then on a fellow soldier's name for him was Socko.

It was also during this time that Bud's love of reading took hold. "A fellow soldier lent me his copy of *The Golden Horde* by LaSelle Gilman. It's still one of my favorites." The book is an epic tale of a soldier's arduous journey across the deserts, mountains and desolate wastes of Mongolia, Russia and China after the Russian Civil War. It delves into relations between disparate cultures, clashes of humanity, and the heritage and ingenuity of the Khans and emperors of earlier times. For Bud, it was an opportunity to escape from the war that was very possibly imminent into another time and place. "That book made me interested in history and larger than life figures. The stories of Genghis Khan fascinated me. He did more with less, and with no formal education, than anyone in history. It made me realize the art of doing the best you can."

THE GOLDEN HORDE,
LASELLE GILMAN'S EPIC NOVEL SPARKED BUD'S INTER-
EST IN HISTORY AND LOVE OF READING.

President Roosevelt signed the extension of the
Burke-Wadsworth Act.

Chapter 3
Protecting the Coast

By the summer of 1941, President Franklin Roosevelt sensed increasing trouble overseas and asked Congress to extend the military duty for those who had come in under the Burke-Wadsworth Act. The ask was easier than the answer. Despite potential and dire consequences for the nation and the world, all those initial draftees wanted at the end of their year of service was out. Their communal cry for release was "O-H-I-O – Over the hill in October."

Approval to keep them in came Aug. 12, 1941, by one vote. It's a margin Bud still finds astonishing. "One vote! Unbelievable! Without that, five national guard divisions, some 100,000 trained soldiers, would have been turned loose, and they would have had real trouble getting us back," he says. "Such isolationism! The Germans were working on bombs and missiles we didn't know about. The Japanese would soon be sending over bomb-carrying balloons on the jet stream to set fire to our forests. The attack on Pearl Harbor had already been planned! We have no idea what would have happened if that vote had gone the other way. It's one of the scariest things in the history of our country, and it's never talked about."

Barely four months later, however, life changed for those in and out of the military. "On Dec. 7, 1941, my sister and I were over at the Vancouver army barracks getting gas (at 13 cents a gallon) for Dad's 1937 Packard 120 when we heard about the attack on Pearl Harbor," Bud recalls. "An announcement came on the car radio that all members of the 41st division were to return to Fort Lewis. So, I quickly drove on up with some other soldiers who'd come down to Portland." Initially, the 41st was put on coast patrol – protecting Oregon and Washington from possible enemy attack from sea or air. "I was the driver for the kitchen truck and was based at Camp Clatsop, now Camp Rilea. We'd transport provisions up to Astoria and down the coast."

THE SOLDIER AND HIS KITCHEN TRUCK.

Such concern turned out to be warranted. The only military installation in the continental United States to come under enemy fire was Fort Stevens, an army base built during the Civil War near the mouth of the Columbia River. Just before midnight June 21, 1942, a Japanese submarine surfaced from the Pacific and fired 17 shells from a deck gun. Not wanting to reveal their position, the fort commander withheld return fire, effectively preventing further engagement. The only damage was to the backstop of the fort's baseball field offering a good story and a tourist attraction for years to come.

By the time of that sneak attack on Fort Stevens, the men of the 41st were long gone.

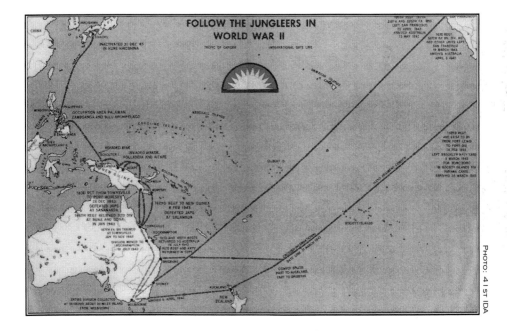

AS A TROOP SHIP, THE *SS MATSONIA* SUPPRESSED THE FRILLS THAT LUXURY CRUISE PASSENGERS EXPECTED.

Chapter 4
Going Down Under

In April of '42, the 186th Infantry Regiment was sent to San Francisco where they boarded the *SS Matsonia* for parts unknown – to them at least. "It wasn't until we got out to sea, probably beyond swimming range," Bud recalls with a chuckle, "that they told us we were going to Australia." Some 5,000 servicemen were on board. Most would not return home for nearly four years.

The 41st held three distinctions. Initially, as a National Guard Division, they were one of the best-trained divisions in the country; they were one of the first shipped out for WWII ground combat; and by eventually being gone from U.S. soil for 45 months, they were destined to serve more time overseas than almost any other U.S. division.

Recommissioned as a troop ship, the *Matsonia*, with the Hawaiian nickname "Maolo" or "flying fish," was a luxury liner that regularly cruised between San Francisco, Los Angeles and Honolulu. For this trip, however, its opulent public rooms, spacious cabins, private lanais, swimming pools, and beauty salons were nowhere to be seen. "It was a lovely ship," Bud says, "but not for us. The food was terrible, we were crammed five guys high and two feet apart in hammocks, and the body odor was intense." Ever looking on the positive side, he adds: "We did have ice cream bars."

For protection on the voyage, the *Matsonia* and her twin ship, the *SS Lurline* also carrying soldiers to Australia, had the *USS Indianapolis*, a flagship of the U.S. Navy's Fifth Fleet. Their zig-zagging path across the ocean to avoid enemy attention allowed the ships a long, uneventful trip. "We didn't see land for 21 days," Bud says. "But we could always see the *Indianapolis* off in the distance. And we saw porpoises, flying fish and lots of stars at night. The constellations were incredible!" Anyone with the respect and appreciation of beauty as Bud could not help but enjoy that part of the journey.

"We all had a soft spot in our hearts for that ship.
All those sailors were on that ship
when it was protecting us."

The *Indianapolis* itself was destined to become a somber symbol of war. Three years after accompanying the *Matsonia* and the *Lurline*, and just after delivering crucial parts for construction of "Little Boy," the Hiroshima-destined atomic bomb, two torpedoes from a Japanese submarine struck the *Indianapolis* as it was en route to the Philippines from Guam. The damaged ship sank in 12 minutes. Of the 1,196 men on board, 317 survived. "We all had a soft spot in our hearts for that ship," Bud says. "All those sailors were on that ship when it was protecting us."

Back in April of '42 on the Australia-bound *Matsonia*, the war was still new and the soldiers were anxious for whatever lie ahead. The main challenge was passing the time; poker was a given. "Lots of money changed hands those days and nights," Bud says. "Three or four men always ended up with the money. They were the skilled players, the con men. Neophytes didn't stand a chance." Not wanting to be involved in something so uncontrollable, Bud stayed away. "There's a degree of enmity, or need for importance and power in that kind of activity, and I just wasn't cut out for it. I'm too conservative."

Sailing was smooth until they reached the Tasman Sea, a 1,200-mile stretch between New Zealand and the southeastern coast of Australia. The area is known for wild weather and raging waters, and many of the men on the *Matsonia* did what few sailors there can avoid, they got sick. And they kept getting sick. "I was OK, but lots of men were throwing up," Bud says. "It was pretty brutal." His memories of that part of the crossing are mainly of cramped quarters, flying fish, card games, and vomit.

And they hadn't even gotten to the war yet.

FEELING THE HEAT

Solid ground waited in Melbourne, as did crowds of cheering, handkerchief-waving Australians. With most of Australia's military off in North Africa fighting Field Marshal Erwin Rommel, Hitler's "Desert Fox," civilians back home felt nearly defenseless. They were anxious for the allied presence and support that arrived by sea.

What the welcoming party on the Melbourne docks lacked was longshoremen to unload the ships. A labor strike left the passenger-soldiers to unload their floating gambling den/sick bay themselves. "At least we knew what we were doing with our gear," Bud says, suggesting that proprietary handling of military goods might have been of value. Plus, after 21 days at sea it gave the men opportunity to get their land legs back.

With gear in tow, their first stop was a vacant military post, Camp Nagambie, about 100 miles north. There they were to ac- climate and resume training. After two months, they moved far- ther north to Rockhampton, Queensland on the coast of the Coral Sea and the edge of the Great Barrier Reef. It was a laborious trip through three Australian states. "The railroad tracks in each state were different. So, we'd go as far as one train could go, get off, un- load our gear, load it onto another train, go as far as that one could go, and do it all over again."

In Rockhampton, they joined other members of the 41st Infantry Division, making them 14,000 members strong, nearly overwhelming the town of 60,000 people. Training intensified, as did the heat. "It was 115 degrees every day, and we were always thirsty," Bud remembers. "The drinking water flowed through above-ground pipes making it almost too hot to drink. But that was all we had."

Along with confronting the heat, the soldiers also had heavy packs to carry. Bud added something important to his: A dictionary. Nestled among his food rations (an assortment of items considered at least better than nothing), mess kit, first aid kit, helmet, and gun (a Springfield star-gauge .30-06 rifle) was his Dictionary of the English Language.

"I read a lot and looked up every word I didn't know," he says. "I have always enjoyed the beauty and power of words. At the time, I found how little I knew. Now I have a good basic vocabulary because of what I did long ago." As to what he read at the time, it included a lot of poetry. "I had taken a college prep class in poetry just before we were called up, so I remember enjoying reading poetry."

At age 22, or 24 by military math, Bud considered himself "straight-forward, and kind of a country boy." Plus, he didn't drink, an attribute that offered opportunity. When the army band needed a bus driver for a short tour of towns around Melbourne, they chose him. "We went all over," he says. "We would stop, set up, the band would play 'Let Me Call You Sweetheart,' and people would buy war bonds. It was fun."

Being the band driver earned him life-long Aussie friends. "On the last night of our tour in Geelong, Victoria, we were invited to stay overnight with people in the town. I stayed with a family that ran the local tourist bureau. When they found out where I was from they brought out travel brochures about Oregon. They fixed a big dinner for me and in the morning served me breakfast in bed!" Over the years, they remained friends and sent gifts when Bud married and his children were born.

AUG. 8, 1942 -
THE DAY BUD BECAME 22 OR, ACCORDING TO THE MILITARY, 24. HANGING BEHIND HIM IS A LYSTER BAG THAT FILTERED AND SANITIZED WATER FOR DRINKING.

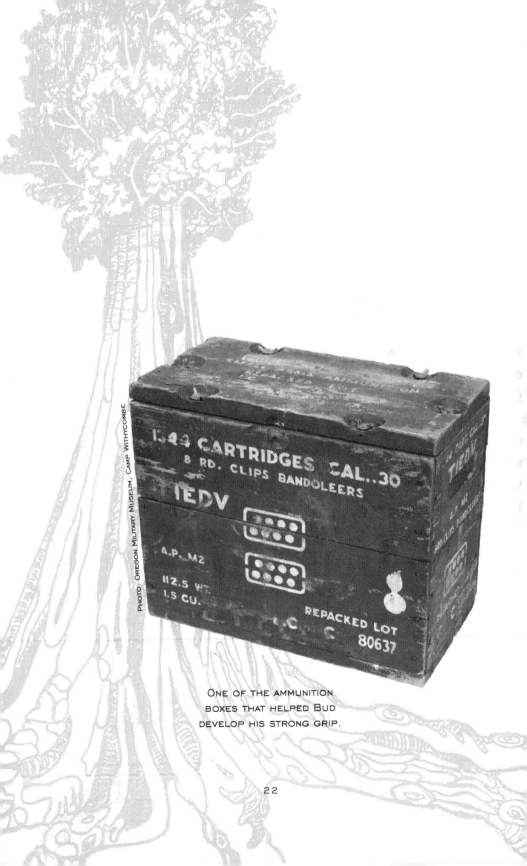

ONE OF THE AMMUNITION
BOXES THAT HELPED BUD
DEVELOP HIS STRONG GRIP.

CHAPTER 5

DEVELOPING THAT GRIP

From band driver, Bud advanced to the regiment's Ammunitions Ordnance Sergeant. In retrospect, it was a solemn reality. "Directly and indirectly I handled every round of ammunition 3,333 soldiers used against the Japanese for two years," he says with some sadness. It was heavy lifting in many ways. His responsibilities included managing and distributing ammunition for all hand guns, rifles, machine guns, submachine guns, light and heavy weapons, 60 mm mortars, 81 mm mortars, and everything that went with it all. The boxes of ammunition, 112.5 pounds each, came without handles. "They just had indentations for your fingers, so to grasp them you carried all the weight on your fingertips. That's why I've always had such strong fingers and a strong grip."

Soon after taking on the ordnance duties, Bud was on his own. Just a short time in, while at Port Moresby, New Guinea, he and his captain were driving in an open jeep near a 90 mm anti-aircraft gun that was aimed to catch incoming bombers. The loud report of the gun when it unexpectedly discharged as they were approaching so startled and scared the captain that Bud immediately thought something must be wrong. "He just about jumped out of the jeep!" It was an indication that indeed something was wrong with the captain. "Not long after that he took a shot at one of our own sentries," Bud remembers. "Nobody got hurt but he was transferred pretty quickly. It was all unfortunate. He was a good man."

Observing

Being in a Service Company, Bud was somewhat detached from combat action. His role, however, gave ample opportunity to observe the rigors of war on those directly involved. Fear was pervasive. "Everyone handles it differently. It doesn't matter who you are, day after day it gets to you. Anyone who says he's not afraid, particularly when bullets are flying and people are screaming and dying, is crazy."

"I knew several soldiers who wouldn't, or couldn't, get out of their foxholes. One was nicknamed 'Fearless.' He was not. But I really couldn't fault him. It's a sure sign of battle fatigue.

"Another fellow froze with a live grenade in his hand. It was during an instruction I was giving on grenade use and showing how to pull the pin and throw the grenade. Well, he pulled the pin and froze. He just stood there! If he'd dropped it, we'd have been playing 52 card pick-up and we'd be being picked up! So as calmly, and as quickly, as I could I got behind him, took his hand and told him he needed to help me throw the grenade as far out in front of us as we could, and he'd need to LET GO! We did that, and he never said a word. Not one word. Very soon he was taken out of a combat position.

"One night late, a captain who I'm convinced was some general's brother-in-law and wanted to see what combat was like, stuck his head into the foxhole I and two other soldiers were in - without giving the sign that he was one of us. It was just dark enough that you had a hard time making things out. We thought he was a Japanese! I could hear one of the other soldiers cocking his rifle. At the same time, I drew my pistol, got my finger on the trigger and was ready to shoot. But at the very, very last second I sensed it was that captain and yelled to the other soldiers not to shoot, and yelled to him to get his ass under a nearby truck and stay there! We were so close to shooting him! The next morning, they found him trying to get into an observation plane that had a range of 500 miles, thinking he'd fly it to Florida! I couldn't blame him. I blame whomever let him be there with us.

"One day, a buddy of mine and I were riding in the back of an open truck and passed under a palm tree. We didn't know it but there was an enemy sniper hiding up there. He must have been waiting for an officer to shoot and just let us go by. We were hardly 75 feet from him. He could have killed us so easily! Our soldiers eventually got him. I don't know how many times that sort of thing took place. The Japanese saw me way more times than I saw them.

"Another day on Biak, we were told a B-25 was coming in to drop us some maps and the plane's bomb bay doors would be open so they could toss them out. Everyone got the message – DO NOT SHOOT AT THE PLANE! IT'S OURS! Then the plane came by and they started tossing out the maps. But when it was right overhead, someone started to shoot. Maybe he thought the Japanese had gotten hold of the plane. Maybe he thought the map canisters coming out were bombs. Maybe he was trigger happy. Maybe he was scared. I don't know, but it was contagious, a dozen other soldiers started shooting, too. The plane erupted in flames with such intense heat! The airmen in the plane, five of them just doing their jobs, were incinerated before they hit the ground a mile away. It's a sad, sad part of war. What would their folks be told? They couldn't be told it was because of our own fire. They'd be told they died bravely. And they did."

Posing on a fallen palm tree on Buna, New Guinea.

26

Chapter 6

Snakes, Spears and Shoes

Second only to Greenland in size, New Guinea is an island with thousands of aboriginal tribes, some of which were discovered just a few years before the outbreak of WWII. "It was like going into another world," Bud says of the natives he encountered. "They were primitive, some even carried spears." U.S. soldiers nicknamed them "Fuzzy Wuzzies" because of their course curly hair. "I didn't call them that because it seemed derogatory and I had too much respect for them. They had amazing skills particularly at sensing, hearing and seeing things we might not notice. That's very important when you live in the jungle."

Some natives had become part of the Royal Papuan Constabulary police force the Australian colonial administration had established in the late 19th century. Ultimately, they played a significant role in helping resist the Japanese in WWII.

Bud's involvement with the natives came after the horrendous and lengthy battle for the Japanese-held beachhead at Buna in late 1942/early 1943. A small village on the eastern tip of Papua, New Guinea, Buna's value was in the airstrip the Japanese had developed there. To capture the airstrip, General Douglas MacArthur had demanded a quick, decisive battle. The 41st Division was best trained and prepared for the action. Sent in instead, however, were parts of the 32nd Division which were positioned nearer to the intended battle site. Although casualty statistics vary, it is estimated that in the fierce two-month battle at Buna, 620 allied soldiers were killed and 2,065 were wounded. On the Japanese side, 1,400 dead were buried. The actual number of Japanese casualties is estimated to be much higher.

At the end of the battle, the 41st Division's 186th Regiment went in to secure the area. Waiting for them were their fellow soldiers who had faced rampant disease, miserable weather, and an enemy that was willing to fight to the death. They severely lacked food, drinking water and ammunition. Of the 32nd Division soldiers he encountered, Bud says, "They looked like they'd been through hell."

HELP AMIDST THE TURMOIL

Swamps, dense jungle, sharp-bladed grasses and ground-covering coral made nearly any move at Buna perilous. The heat hovered around 120 degrees. The rain was constant at nearly 10 inches every day. And the enemy bombing raids continued.

As the ammunitions sergeant, Bud's job was to collect and salvage ammunition the 32nd Division had left behind. "I had two strings of native constabularies helping me. They did a good job. Some could speak pidgin English so we communicated pretty well." Christmas carols though, came as a surprise. "One of the natives started singing 'Silent Night' and others joined in. We figured missionaries had taught them the songs." It all seemed incongruous, Bud remembers. "Here we were in the middle of the jungle and the natives were singing a Christmas carol!"

Also incongruous, was the time he and another soldier, both very thirsty, walked through a native village, found the chief and, through stumbling pantomiming, asked for water. "We held out our canteens, and the chief immediately sent some young boys off to fill them." That's when the two soldiers realized they were standing amidst a group of natives, perhaps 10 to 12 in all, bearing spears. Sharp spears.

"Let's say we were apprehensive," Bud recalls with a chuckle. "They weren't menacing. We knew they were on our side, but here we were, soldiers from a modern army standing among warriors practically from the stone age. We had our guns, but they had spears, and there were more of them than there were of us!" To their relief, the boys with the water showed up shortly and Bud and his fellow modern gun-holder continued on their way. Quickly.

When the opportunities arose, Bud of course, made friends with the natives. One young boy of about 14 nearly became his friend for life. "The boy was helping us move some ammunition and picked up a load of shells that was too heavy for him," he remembers. "His knees began to buckle and he almost collapsed before I got over to get it. He was so grateful that from then on he brought me bananas, coconuts, oranges, pineapples. Wherever I was, he'd find me. I finally had to tell him I was fine and he could stop!"

Also native to the area were snakes, common death adders being the more prevalent. Appropriately named due to the lack of a ready antidote to their poison, a death adder hides under leaves and twitches its tail to lure unsuspecting prey. Anything that comes to inspect the movement gets a quick bite and an injection of venom. The snake then waits for the victim's quick death, and eats it.

"I almost stepped on one once," Bud remembers quite vividly. "A native saw it, yelled, grabbed a stick and killed it. Another time, I was stacking ammunition boxes, looked down and saw one coiled right on the box. He was about 4 feet long, mean looking, with a big face like a wolf. Good thing I looked first! I took a stick, hit him as hard as I could several times and killed him. It wasn't easy! Either time I'd have been dead so fast, and nothing could have been done."

From Buna, Bud's division moved on to other areas where conditions were basically the same – swampy, disease-prone, snake-ridden, insect-infested, and lacking drinkable water. "We always drank from our bags of purified water," he says. "One time, I was tempted to drink out of what looked like a clean stream but then I saw a body floating in it. So, I didn't."

The island of Biak which is comprised mostly of coral and jungle was the site of one of the bloodiest battles in the Pacific theater. Too few U.S. soldiers fighting too many Japanese soldiers nearly guaranteed a loss. "The Japanese were already dug in – in caves, in tunnels, on cliffs overlooking our landing area, everywhere," Bud remembers.

Achieving victory took from May through August 1944. With it, the entire 41st Division earned a new nickname previously given only to the 162nd Regiment of the division, the "Jungleers." Despite being nearly outnumbered three-to-one by Japanese troops, their efforts resulted in capture of three airstrips and a staging area on the island that were valuable to future operations. On the U.S. mainland, the greater focus was on the war in Europe. The June 6, 1944 Invasion of Normandy overshadowed the Biak campaign. Nevertheless, it was a crucial and hard-fought victory.

For Bud, Biak was also the site of a nearly lethal encounter with military shoes – replacements for those the coral on the island quickly ripped through. Always chuckling at the memory, he says, "The headline in the newspaper back home would have read: 'Sergeant Leland S. Lewis dies bravely fighting the Japanese.' That's all they could have said!" The story was that Bud was out waiting for a B-17 supply plane to drop the replacement shoes – thousands of pairs in hundreds of cartons. But without warning, the pilot extended the drop zone and the cartons started coming straight down toward the jeep Bud was sitting in. "I looked up, saw those cartons hurtling toward me at what must have been 100 miles an hour, jumped out as fast as I could and ran under a coconut tree. Good thing. A carton crushed the jeep's steering wheel and destroyed the dashboard! Other drops tore through communication lines and smashed up the whole area!"

Having avoided the "friendly fire," Bud's family and the hometown crowd were saved from mourning his demise as a hero of the war. "Think of it!" he says incredulously. "Shoes!"

Throughout his time in the South Pacific, Bud was in the enlisted ranks. When the chance to become an officer arose, he jumped at it. The fact it did not work out is a quirk of fate he believes that helped keep him alive.

In April 1944, while in Rockhampton, he and another enlistee were summoned to Officer Candidate School and scheduled to leave their posts for training in Brisbane. "Just before we were to leave, it was cancelled. The higher ups decided to use the personnel they already had. We were really disappointed."

Despite the disappointment, the decision was likely of lasting value. "I'm big and would have stood out. If I'd had a platoon to lead I would have had to set an example, and that would have made me a target." Not being an officer allowed him to go home as a staff sergeant, and alive. But just barely.

DRAWING: DIANE LEWIS

GENGHIS KHAN, 1162 - 1227,
THE FOUNDER OF THE MONGOL
EMPIRE (ALSO A TARGET FOR
MALARIA-CARRYING MOSQUITOES).

CHAPTER 7
BATTLING DISEASE

A malaria-carrying mosquito bit Genghis Khan. One also got Alexander the Great, Christopher Columbus, Napoleon, George Washington, Abraham Lincoln, Mother Teresa, Ho Chi Minh, and endless numbers of people - known and unknown. Bud Lewis was bitten, too. Twice.

"The first time, was when we were scheduled for amphibious training out of Brisbane. I missed the training because I wasn't feeling well. A friend of mine whose brother-in-law back home was a pharmacist (he had MORE stuff!) had a thermometer and took my temperature. It was 104 degrees." The temperature qualified Bud for a trip to the nearest field hospital. "It was the worst ride of my life! The hospital was 70 miles away on bumpy, pitted, rutted, barely drivable roads. It was awful." In the hospital for two weeks, Bud lost 20 pounds. "When I got back, they called me Bones."

Like those many before, Bud had been bitten by the scourge of warfare - modern and ancient. Speculation is that in 452 AD Attila the Hun could not invade Rome because too many of his men were sick with malaria. In 1781, the British surrender at Yorktown and the conclusion of the Revolutionary War was likely due to malaria having devastated the British forces. In WWII, U.S. servicemen in the South Pacific suffered eight times as many casualties from malaria as from combat. The disease presents as cycles of fever, uncontrollable shivering, headache, profuse sweating, nausea and muscle pain that become an internal war joining whatever external one might be raging.

The other downside is that even with Atabrine, malaria prevention was not 100 percent.

Attempting to quell the disease, the U.S. military turned to Atabrine, a drug developed in the 1930s by a German researcher. A stiff potion in yellow pills, Atabrine was given to all troops in the South Pacific. Taking it was mandatory despite the fact it tasted awful, turned the skin yellow, caused headaches, nausea, vomiting and, in a few cases, temporary psychosis. "They watched us take it," Bud says. "You couldn't play games like put it under your tongue and spit it out." The other downside is that even with Atabrine, malaria prevention was not 100 percent.

Bud's second bout with malaria was on Biak. "I got the shakes and the chills and was sent right away to an island hospital for two weeks. Then I went back to my unit, and a month later got hepatitis."

Infectious hepatitis has also been a common side effect of warfare through the ages. It comes from contaminated food and water. Serum hepatitis, another WWII scourge, was caused by contaminated vaccines. Symptoms for both strains were similar and much like malaria – fever, chills, fatigue, nausea, loss of appetite, abdominal pain, and often, inflammation of the liver which brought a yellow tinge to the skin and eyes.

For Bud, infectious hepatitis was his ticket home. But he didn't know it, and he didn't really want it. The first place it put him was on the hospital ship *USS Comfort* to rest and recuperate. The U.S. military operated 24 hospital ships in the European and Pacific theaters during WWII. Most were refitted and recommissioned passenger, cargo, freighter, or troopships. The *Comfort*, however, was a new hospital and convalescent ship, and entered service in May of 1944 with onboard facilities for 400 patients.

"I'll never forget that ship," Bud says of his week on board. "It was so clean and white. They had everything. Even ice cream!" Unfortunately, because he was so sick, Bud could eat very little - not the ice cream and certainly not the Crab Louie's that crept into his dreams.

Then, and now, hospital ships are protected under Principles of the Geneva Convention's "Adaption to Maritime Warfare" agreed upon in 1907. Those principles made it a crime to attack a hospital ship. Both Japan and Germany ratified that agreement. By WWII, however, neither were signatories to it.

Seven months after Bud's time on the *USS Comfort*, a kamikaze pilot dove his plane straight into the ship, crashing through three decks and exploding in a surgery room filled with doctors, nurses and patients. Seven hundred people were on the ship when the attack came; 28 were killed and 48 were wounded.

After release from the *Comfort*, Bud was sent to the general hospital in Milne Bay, New Guinea. There he was told his time in the South Pacific was over and he would be going home. "I really didn't want to go," he says. "I wanted to stay with my unit. I'd just been promoted to staff sergeant and we were about to go to the Philippines."

It was a sad departure. "I gave my pistol, a beautiful .45 caliber 1911, to the soldier who replaced me. It was an historic, very efficient gun. It could put a hole through you like a broom handle," Bud says with a twinkle in his eye. "Wish I'd kept it!"

HOMEWARD BOUND

The *USS Republic*, a troop transport that had many previous lives including as a merchant ship, a cargo ship, and a passenger liner took Bud home. It was a slow single stacker. The voyage to San Francisco took 20 days and included a layover in Honolulu for food and fuel. There, the excitement was the radio broadcasts of the 1944 World Series. Dubbed the "Streetcar Series," it was a showdown between the St. Louis Cardinals and the St. Louis Browns, both of which claimed Sportsman's Park of St. Louis, Missouri, as their home field. Despite the military having drafted away many of baseball's star players, and teams across the country putting in their second, third and fourth strings, the games were an attraction – particularly to sports fans like Bud who were hungry for diversion that put competitors on the ball field and not the battlefield.

"I couldn't leave the ship so I listened to the games on the ship's radio," he says. "But that was OK, I got to hear about my favorite players." And those were left-handed Cardinal pitcher Harry "The Cat" Brecheen and Cardinal outfielder/first baseman "Stan the Man" Musial. Bud, of course, did not have money on the game. Perhaps he should have. His players came out on top with the Cardinals besting the Browns 4-2.

Several lengthy, state-side hospital stays were in the cards for Bud before good health returned. But it did, as did he to Portland, his family, and a budding romance that had begun back before the *Matsonia* set sail to Australia.

His discharge from active duty came Sept. 3, 1945 at Fort Lewis at age 25 (by then his real age and his military age had reached agreement).

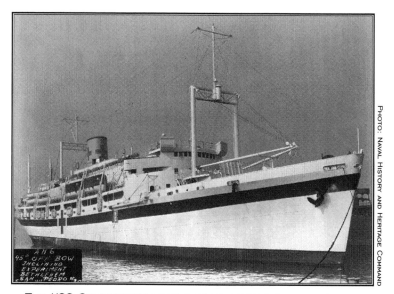

THE *USS COMFORT* WAS BOTH A COMFORT TO SICK AND WOUNDED SOLDIERS AND A VICTIM OF WAR.

JANET. BUD WAS TAKEN BY HER BEAUTY.

Chapter 8
Noticing Her Beauty

"She was beautiful, and wore the most lovely perfume."

That's what attracted Bud when he first met Janet Spencer at a friend's house – her beauty and her scent. (To be honest, he was also attracted by the friend's '38 Buick. "Nice car!" he remembers.) It was July of '41 and Bud was on a weekend pass from Fort Lewis. "Oh my God, she was just beautiful! I liked her right away," he says (of Janet). "But I didn't let her know, I was kind of bashful."

At the time, the beautiful and aromatic Janet was going with another fellow, but Bud was not too bashful to get her telephone number and invite her out when he was on another leave. That's when they found out they shared birthdays, Aug. 8. As Leos, it was a commonality to help foster a relationship.

Unfortunately, soldiering left little opportunity to invest in a relationship, particularly when war was imminent and Bud's unit was sent off to the South Pacific. Letters had to take the place of presence and to compete with the other fellow in Janet's life. "Mostly we wrote about what was going on. I told her how hot the weather was and she told me about her job at an insurance company in Portland."

Bud valued the correspondence both as a way to fan the embers back home and to ward off local ladies who might see him as an eventual ticket out of Australia. "I have a sweetheart back home," he could say. Sometimes he even fudged a bit and said he was "engaged to a lovely lady in Portland," which, though not yet true, could get him off any local hooks. "I really didn't want to get involved with anyone else," he says.

He did not, and neither did she. After returning from the South Pacific and recovering from the hepatitis that sent him home, Bud started seeing Janet in earnest. They became engaged in early Feb. 1945 and married Oct. 13, 1945.

Elegant and artistic, Janet was the more subdued of the couple. "Mom knew what she was getting into," says daughter Diane. "She often told the story of Dad waving and stopping to chat with guests as they went back down the aisle at their wedding." Janet grew to accommodate Bud's ability to make friends everywhere by becoming very well read. "She always had a book with her," Diane says, "to pass the time when Dad was visiting."

The couple's first home was an apartment in Northwest Portland. With the addition of children, Doug in '48 and Diane in '50, they moved to a house in Northeast Portland, and finally to a home below Council Crest with a sweeping view toward the coast with flowers and foliage that attract hummingbirds, blue jays, crows, doves, chickadees, wrens, and whatever else might pass by.

Bud and Janet were married nearly 68 years. Janet passed away Jan. 26, 2013.

"One of the best things I ever did was marry Janet Spencer," Bud says. "She was such a decent, lovely woman."

"A RED, RED ROSE"

O my Luve is like a red, red rose
That's newly sprung in June;
O my Luve is like the melodie
That's sweetly play'd in tune.

As fair art thou, my bonie lass,
So deep in luve am I;
And I will luve thee still, my dear,
Till a' the seas gang dry.

Till a' the seas gang dry, my dear,
And the rocks melt wi' the sun;
I will luve thee still, my dear,
While the sands o' life shall run.

And fare thee weel, my only luve,
And fare thee weel a while!
And I will come again, my luve,
Tho it were ten thousand mile!

by Robert Burns, 1794

"Ozymandias"

I met a traveler from an antique land
Who said: Two vast and trunkless legs of stone
Stand in the desert... Near them, on the sand,
Half sunk, a shattered visage lies, whose frown,
And wrinkled lip, and sneer of cold command,
Tell that its sculptor well those passions read
Which yet survive, stamped on these lifeless things,
The hand that mocked them and the heart that fed:
And on the pedestal these words appear:
"My name is Ozymandias, king of kings:
Look on my works, ye Mighty, and despair!"
Nothing beside remains. Round the decay
Of that colossal wreck, boundless and bare
The lone and level sands stretch far away.

by Percy Bysshe Shelley, 1818

CHAPTER 9
SHARING THE JOY OF POETRY

"It reminds me of a poem. . ." He might not even say that. Spurred by the conversation, or an inspirational sight, he might just begin reciting. A short poem, a long poem, a sonnet. Verbatim.

It's a skill Bud developed while taking night classes at Portland Community College (and walking a beat as a police officer during the day). Ten Modern American Poets was the class that continued his interest in poetry following a class he had taken before going off to war. His specific focus was Emily Dickinson. "I was intrigued by her because of her writing style. She could do more with less," he says. "That shows great talent."

A later class featured a film presentation of poets discussing works that interested them. It was Maya Angelou's delivery of "Ozymandias" that solidified Bud's desire to memorize. "She recited that sonnet of Percy Shelley and I thought she was wonderful, and I thought it was wonderful to know a piece that well. I decided right then I had to memorize that poem and others."

The value of memorizing, Bud believes, "Is that you can keep verbal expressions of beauty in your mind, in the very front of your being, and bring them out whenever you want."

In addition to Emily Dickinson and Percy Shelley, a list of Bud's favorite poets includes Edgar Allan Poe, Elizabeth Barrett Browning, Robert Browning, Robert Burns, Alfred Edward Housman, and Edward FitzGerald's translation of "The Rubaiyat of Omar Khayyam."

On the job in 1946.

Chapter 10
Serving as One of Portland's Finest

Honesty, being one of Bud's most basic characteristics, compels him to explain why a career in police or fire-fighting work beckoned him. "I could say I wanted to help people. But that would be garbage. I was interested because the pay was $186 a month. Before the military, I had been making $80 a month steaming furniture at Doernbecher Manufacturing Company. It was definitely the pay."

It all started Sept. 13, 1941 when the 186th Service Company was still based at Fort Lewis. Bud had gone to Portland on a pass and had a decision to make. Should he take the Portland Police Bureau entrance exam in the morning and the fire fighter exam in the afternoon or take the police exam in the morning and go on a date with his sister's friend in the afternoon?

He was 21. The morning exam and the afternoon date won out.

Looking back over his 31 years with the police bureau, the decision turned out to be a good one. The girl was not a keeper but he passed the police exam with flying colors and, after those five years of military service, he embarked on a positive, eventful career with the bureau. The pay took him to the job, but the people, opportunities, and adventure kept him there.

After recovering from the hepatitis that had brought him home from the South Pacific, Bud still had five months' service to complete. With good fortune, he was assigned to be Commander of the Guard at the Portland Army Airbase. The position connected closely with Police Bureau activities and allowed him to become familiar with their personnel and procedures – all of which were helpful when he officially joined.

In September of 1945, he traded in his military khakis for police blues, handcuffs, a Smith & Wesson .38 caliber Chief's Special revolver, and a sap – a leather covered wooden night stick for subduing unruly citizens who might need close-range subduing. The pay was $227 a month.

His first post was a day shift walking beat through downtown Portland. For a while, he was on the midnight to 8 a.m. shift. "That was the second night shift," he says. "Lots of rowdy stuff goes on at that time of night. But I got to know people in nearly every building down there. And I like to think I was always fair and treated everyone like a lady or a gentleman." On the flip side, he allows that if their response was not cordial, "that was their problem." When necessary, backup came after contacting headquarters from a police call box or from a phone at a convenient tavern, café or store.

With his military and street experience, Bud gained the confidence to approach any situation that arose, particularly when teaming up with a cadre of his trusted fellow patrolmen. "We'd go into a tavern of 50 or 60 people and know we could handle whatever might be going on," he says. Stature, courage and their desire to reduce conflict to a manageable level, he believes is what made them effective. "I could be firm if needed, but that's not my nature. Our presence was really the most important."

That presence shone through on a New Year's Eve when he and a fellow patrolman responded to a call about a loud, obnoxious drunk who was drawing a crowd. "The man was a windbag and a bully," Bud recalls. To quell the disturbance, they arrested him and set off to the central precinct's jail.

Despite the escort of two patrolmen, the drunk's taunts and jeers continued. By the time they reached the jail, Bud had enough. "I knew he was really just a cowardly big mouth," he says. So, Bud decided he and his inebriated arrestee should ride in the elevator to the fifth-floor jail together, just the two of them. And indeed, the ride confirmed the cowardice. As to what took place in the elevator, Bud won't divulge except to stress the lack of any police brutality. "I just taught him a lesson," he says with a smile, "in a genteel sort of way."

BE PREPARED

In his 31 years as a Portland Police officer, Bud is proud to say he only took his Smith & Wesson .38 out twice. "I told that to a patrolman a while ago and he said that's done much more frequently now." He quickly points out, however, that gun use reflects the needs of the times, and that 18 years of his service were in positions that did not require use of such force. The reality of using a gun as a police officer, he emphasizes, is using it correctly and only when truly necessary. "Nevertheless, when the need arises," he says, "unless you're ready to offer yourself up as a target, you have to be prepared and ready to use it."

Both times of un-holstering his .38 were when he was investigating burglaries – alone. Both were at taverns and neither time did the burglars, two in each case, have or show weapons. "If they'd had guns though, I would have used the necessary force," Bud says. "But they were young and scared. Nothing happened, except in one case one of them wet his pants."

As to the sap, "Never had the need for it."

Being prepared and doing what was necessary to minimize the situation were keys to Bud's style of handling tricky situations. Take the evening he was returning to the central precinct and noticed a man, a civilian, attempting to direct traffic along Front Avenue (today's Naito Parkway). Bud stopped his car nearby to watch what was going on. The man saw him, walked over, pointed to the blue uniform and said, "That's the color of the Lord," to which Bud thought, "Uh oh, I've got a live one."

"It took four officers to subdue him and they had to put him in a padded cell!"

Hearing the car's motor, the man said it was the "sound of the Lord." "Yes," Bud agreeably responded, "Isn't that beautiful?" Not knowing what the fellow might do, Bud considered his approach. "I figured we were becoming friends and he was trusting me, so I said I would hate for him to get hurt out there in traffic, and asked if I could take him to the hospital where they could help if something was bothering him."

The new friend agreed, and sensing the fellow was probably harmless, Bud got him into the car but set off instead for the emergency hospital at the jail thinking that any problem could be handled best there. On arrival, he explained the situation as mildly as he could and left the man with intake officers.

And then the sparks flew.

"The man went berserk!" Bud remembers being told. "It took four officers to subdue him and then they had to put him in a padded cell!"

Another memorable encounter that turned after Bud left, involved a drunk driver he came upon just before a Rose Festival parade. "I arrested him, and sent him off in the wagon to jail." A surprise was in store. Soon after Bud put him in the system, the prisoner took himself out becoming the only inmate, up to that time, to break out of the Portland City Jail. "It turned out he had a hacksaw blade taped between his shoulders. No handle, just the blade. I hadn't seen any need to frisk him when I arrested him and apparently neither did anyone else." After being put in a cell, the man sobered up enough to un-tape the blade, saw through the bars on the window, climb onto the ledge, and crawl down the fire escape.

"I suspect he had some outstanding warrants and didn't want to be found out. Or," Bud adds with a chuckle, "maybe he just wanted to see the parade. But whomever sold the city on that jail being escape-proof, sold them a bill of goods!"

And then there was a potentially violent altercation during a union strike in the early 1960s. The police were called to help at an event where unionized members of Portland's daily newspapers were gathered. "I was the sergeant on duty and took eight or 10 other officers with me," he recalls. "When we got there, one striker took ahold of my tie and tried to choke me!" What happened next was likely regrettable from the tie-grabbers viewpoint, "I got my tie back and put him in jail."

Bud's police work sometimes included assignments to the intelligence division. One involved protecting the president of a local bank whose life had been threatened. His role in that case was surveillance – watching, following, and essentially shadowing the bank president when he was in public.

And for the shortest time in the history of the police bureau, he was a detective. Bud's brief stint in the position was due to his desire to continue with his college education enabled through the new G.I. Bill that provided educational benefits for those who had served in the military. Knowing he couldn't do well in both a new job assignment and at evening school, he turned down the detective opportunity and continued his time on the streets while he also pursued courses in Police Science.

"Community Policing" aptly defines Bud's approach to the assignments he undertook and the way he performed them. Each post gave him broad exposure throughout the city with an increasing understanding of people of all types and in all kinds of situations. "It's important to remember," he says, "that the officers on the street are on their own. They're the ones who make the decisions about whether to use necessary force. They're the ones who work to save others. It takes experience, maturity, intelligence, and a lot of courage."

REGRETS

Two regrets of those street beat years seem either odd or highly fitting when considering the love of beauty and the gregariousness of Bud Lewis. "I never went into the old Portland Hotel," he says. "I'm told it was beautiful inside. I wish I'd taken an

PHOTO: OREGON HISTORICAL SOCIETY

KNOWN AS "THE PORTLAND," THE HOTEL WAS THE SOCIAL AND ARCHITECTURAL CENTER OF THE CITY FROM 1890 TO 1951.

opportunity to go in to see." Built in the late 19th century heyday of grand, opulent hotels, the Portland Hotel reigned over the city on what is now Pioneer Courthouse Square. Its lavish elegance made it the place to see and be seen. Presidents, celebrities and other luminaries stayed there. By 1951 though, time had gotten the better of the hotel and it was taken down. The grounds became a parking lot and remained so for nearly 30 years.

And then, there was Theodore Penland. "I never spent any time talking with him," Bud laments. Well-known as a veteran of the Civil War, Penland was the last surviving member of the Grand Army of the Republic, a fraternal organization of Union Army veterans. He died in 1950 at age 101. Originally from Indiana, his later years were spent holding court on a bench at Portland's Greyhound Bus Station on S.W. Fifth and Taylor talking with friends and passersby about his war experiences, his

THEODORE AUGUSTUS PENLAND, 1849 - 1950

work on the transcontinental railroad, and life in general. "Imagine who he must have seen and met," Bud muses. "Grant? Sherman? Lincoln? I often saw him there but never had the chance to sit and talk. I wish I had."

TONITE Channel 6

PORTLAND
WRESTLING
LIVE!
FROM THE ARMORY
10:05 P.M.

Channel 6

CHAPTER 11

PLAYING A SUPPORTING ROLE

In the 1950s and '60s, some of the best theater in town was at the Portland Armory, and Bud Lewis played an important supporting role. Renovated and repurposed into today's Gerding Theater, the Portland Armory at N.W. 10th and Couch is the very building where Bud drilled with the Oregon National Guard in the 1930s. Twenty and 30 years later, it was also where professional wrestling matches took place every Friday night, 10 to 11 p.m., January through December. Bud, off duty but in full police uniform with full police authority, was the security officer. His employer during those hours was the wrestling promoter who wanted him there to ensure the fights stayed inside the ring. This was a job not just anyone could handle, especially when the fans were hungry for power and muscle, and the wrestlers were doing their best to serve it up.

Fight nights brought some 500 people crowding into the Armory with thousands more tuning in on television. In those days of live TV, Portland was a hot spot for wrestling. It was where new talent came to develop their on-camera skills and tried-and-true talent came to hone their repertoire of theatrical responses. A traveling cast of "good guys" and "bad guys" appeared weekly. Figures such as Rowdy Roddy Piper, Playboy Buddy Rose, Mad

Dog Vachon, Haru Sasaki, Kurt von Poppenheim, Shag Thomas, Lonnie Mayne, and Dutch Savage did their best to ignite crowd passion and arouse lusty cheers and jeers.

As a constant presence, Bud, looming large and imposing, was almost as well-known and recognized as the wrestlers. "For years, people would come up to me on the street, call me by name, and say they'd seen me on television at the matches," he says. Intentionally or not, he was part of the show.

Among his duties was ensuring the wrestlers got safely to and from the ring. At the start and finish of each match, attendees and home-viewers would roar as the wrestlers pranced or strutted down the aisle, leering or ogling at the crowd. Close behind was blue-uniformed Bud Lewis who, at 6 feet 3½ inches, easily towered over his charges.

"I'd have to be in lock-step with those guys.
I never knew what they or the fans might do."

On any given Friday, he might escort muscle-bound Haru Sasaki, the "Japanese Boogeyman," demonstrating his trademark karate chops, or the equally muscular Kurt von Poppenheim with curled mustache, clipped goatee and left-eye monocle, sporting a robe emblazoned with an iron cross. "I'd have to be in lock-step with those guys," Bud says. "I never knew what they or the fans might do."

To stimulate audience reaction, the wrestlers had their fits and tantrums ready to display as opportunities arose. Bud recalls wrestler Eric Pedersen emerging one night from behind the curtain looking crazed. " 'Bud,' he told me, 'I'm going on the floor,' and I'd think, Oh, God, here we go again, but I'd say, 'I'll be right behind you.' Then he'd bug out his eyes, grab a chair, bang it into another chair, and stuff would fly!"

Knowing it was all for entertainment, Bud had to temper his policing style to the occasion. "I had to be a little different there than out on the street," he says. "I wouldn't allow anything physical in the audience but there was a lot of language I would just have to let go."

Not just fun and games

As with his police work, much of this work was done through sheer force of presence. It's what slowed impassioned fans from attempting to be part of the show by perhaps burning a villainous wrestler with a cigarette butt as he strode by or sticking him with a hat pin (the weapon-of-choice for some women at the time). Once in a while a fan would think it fun to hit someone with a pellet from a well-aimed sling shot, but Bud would quickly put an end to it.

Nevertheless, things could have gotten out of hand easily, especially when the wrestlers took their act into the crowd. "They were masters at inciting the crowd," Bud remembers. "I had to make sure no mob mentality took over." Those were also the days when smoking was allowed inside but drinking was not. This meant alcohol was consumed before the matches. The occasionally inebriated fans, however, did not bother him. "If it became a problem, I'd tell them they had to leave or they'd go to jail."

One particular evening the passions of one fan grew too high. "I had my eye on a man whose excitement was just building and building. He really should not have been there. I tried to get over to him and to say 'Friend, don't get so wrapped up in this.' But before I could he collapsed." The fan was taken out quietly and died of a heart attack on the way to the hospital.

"It was all a study in human psychology," Bud says of those in the crowd. "Wrestling fans come from all walks of life. I could stereotype and say they were emotionally immature, but I'm not sure there was a common denominator. There were many good folks there, good citizens. Some just wanted and needed an outlet."

"I told him I didn't care how tough he was if he didn't act like a gentleman I'd show him how."

As to those in the ring, "They were fine athletes and entertainers, and were exciting to watch." Despite appearing as fierce enemies, most were friends and cordial to each other, and to Bud, too. "They appreciated what I did and respected me," he says remembering only once having trouble with a wrestler. "He was doing some stuff that really could have incited a riot – yelling and swearing at people," Bud says. "I told him I didn't care how tough he was if he didn't act like a gentleman I'd show him how." With the other wrestlers also putting in a few words, the trouble quickly stopped.

Although he was not officially on duty at the matches, Bud could have made arrests of wrestlers or attendees but doesn't recall ever needing to control anyone's actions to that extent. His presence, stature and demeanor were enough.

After 10 years, Bud left the wrestling gig when his son's high school basketball schedule began to conflict with the wrestling schedule.

A team of four security guards was needed to fill his shoes.

PHOTO: OREGON JOURNAL/OREGON HISTORICAL SOCIETY

PORTLAND ARMORY, CIRCA 1968.
IN THE '50S AND '60S THE BUILDING WAS A WRESTLING VENUE.

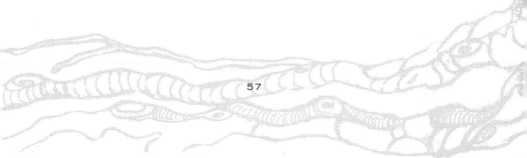

Bud with his Safety Education team.

Chapter 12

Teaching Safety

Part way through his time as wrestling security, Bud's day job changed. From downtown walking-beat cop, he advanced to skating partner for elementary school children. And he loved it. His new realm was the Police Bureau's Safety Education unit where he became director. "They wanted someone who was young and fairly articulate. It was an important job and I felt privileged to be in it," he says.

"I got to know every superintendent,
almost every principal, many parents,
and thousands and thousands of kids."

With a small team of officers, Bud's unit worked throughout the Portland School District's nearly 100 buildings and 52,000 students. Their focus was on all forms of traffic safety – pedestrian, bicycle, and driving. "We got involved as much as we could," he says. "I got to know every superintendent, almost every principal, many parents, and thousands and thousands of kids." Indeed, seeing and being seen within the student, parent and school communities was important to him and his team, as was joining in at the annual skating party for students who participated in the safety patrol program at their schools. "Safety patrol was and is an important way to involve kids in keeping their schools safe," he says. "Kids continue to get a lot out of that responsibility."

In the high schools, the unit's attention was on driver safety. A program for sophomores included illustrating the length of time it takes for a car to stop. A special device attached to the test car's bumper would blow out powder to show the driver's reaction time and the stopping distance. Results, Bud found, were often gender-based. "Boys would find out they couldn't stop as fast as they thought. At that age, boys think they know everything, but they don't," he says. "Girls did a much better job."

"The schools appreciated our officers," Bud recalls. "It all made for good relations between the police bureau and the public. People still tell me they remember me from being in their schools a long time ago. I love it!"

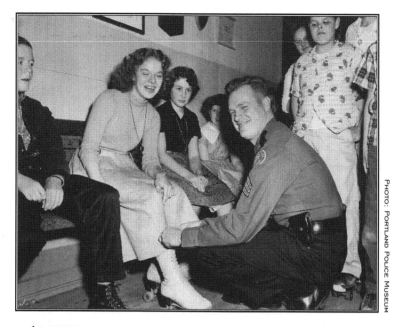

PHOTO: PORTLAND POLICE MUSEUM

AN ANNUAL SKATING PARTY WAS THE OPPORTUNITY FOR STUDENTS AND SAFETY EDUCATION UNIT OFFICERS TO CELEBRATE THE CITY-WIDE SAFETY PATROL PROGRAM.

CHAPTER 13

INSTRUCTING THE RULES OF THE ROAD

"**S**gt. Lewis taught me to drive." Multiply that by hundreds and it might approach the number of Portland teenagers Bud taught to drive between the mid-1950s and the mid-1970s. Were the streets of Portland safer because of him? Undoubtedly.

It started with a phone call to the Police Bureau's Traffic Division that then-Sgt. Bud Lewis happened to answer. A father was looking for a police officer who could teach his son to drive. As director of the Bureau's Safety Education unit, it seemed the natural thing for Bud to do, so he offered himself up.

From that grew Defensive Driving Techniques, Bud's off-hours, licensed venture that attracted anxious parents and excited students, all finding it and him by word-of-mouth. Evenings and weekends, when the opportunities arose and time allowed, Bud guided young would-be drivers through empty parking lots, starting and stopping, turning left and right, shifting up, down, forward and reverse. As skills advanced, they drove on deserted streets, up and down hills stopping and starting mid-way, they parallel and front-in parked, stopped at crosswalks, navigated in-tersections, and figured out how to manage skids by turning in rather than away. Soon-to-be licensees learned how to handle a car and to be safe behind the wheel with finesse and expertise.

"I was very serious about it," he says. "I tried to impress on them that if you're going to drive a car, you have to accept the responsibility."

Teaching had its challenges. Since lessons took place in the student's or their parents' car there were no handy passenger-side dual controls, as some instructors had, to stomp on or grab when things got tense or a wayward turn was imminent. Was Bud ever anxious about what the student might do as he or she attempted to pilot a nearly two-ton gasoline-powered machine, that could easily be likened to a loaded weapon, across a roadway?

"Absolutely!" he says. "They were kids! But I never let on. That would have scared them, and it wouldn't have helped. I got pretty good at being nervy, and not showing any anxiety."

"I'm sure he realized that I and his other students would someday be out on the road and he wanted us to know what we were doing."

Past driving student Diane Davies Hussey remembers lessons with Bud as a painstaking yet positive experience. "I'm sure he realized that I and his other students would someday be out on the road and he wanted us to know what we were doing," she says. "He was serious, but he never lost his temper or seemed scared."

"I wanted them to understand that they needed to be thoughtful and careful," Bud says. He found that message particularly important to impress on his male students. "When you're driving," he remembers saying "the life of everyone in your car is in your hands. Don't do something foolish just to try to be impressive. If you want to show off, do it at school or in athletics, not in a car."

Ed Tonkin, middle son of well-known Portland auto dealer Ron Tonkin, remembers his introduction to instructor Sgt. Lewis well. "I was 15 years old and this big, imposing man showed up at our house. I was scared to death!"

I think my mom found Sgt. Lewis. Little did I know what a warm, lovely man he was. But looking at him then, I was nervous as hell!"

That fear was well-founded. In his early teenage years, young Eddy worked at his father's car lots, washing cars and running errands for the sales staff. His habit of commandeering the dealerships' sportier, more powerful vehicles (think the Chevrolet muscle cars – Corvettes, Chevelles, El Caminos,) and racing them around the back lot preceded Bud's arrival at the Tonkin home. ("What can I say?" the now matured Ed confesses, "Cars are in my blood.") With too much frequency, the joy rides resulted in damage to the car being driven and to assorted vehicles parked throughout the lot. One day, having had enough, the lot's exasperated manager grabbed the errant heir, marched him into the head office and exclaimed "Ron! Eddy is smashing up our inventory! It's got to stop!"

"I think my mom found Sgt. Lewis," Ed says. "Little did I know what a warm, lovely man he was. But looking at him then, I was nervous as hell!"

Safety and obeying the rules of the road were key to Bud's teaching method. "It was, 'You're going to do it the way I tell you to do it,'" Ed recalls, "'And, you're going to keep doing it until you do it right and on your own.'" The technique must have had staying power because students of Defensive Driving Techniques always passed the drivers' test the first time.

The success of his students and his enjoyment in teaching them put Bud at a crossroads. Should he develop the business which would have been lucrative and could have quickly eclipsed his work with the police department? Or should he continue offering lessons when time allowed? His love for police work, particularly with the Safety Education Unit, and the realization that expanding would have meant needing to hire other instructors and losing the personal touch he enjoyed, helped make the decision to stay small and sporadic.

Through the years, Bud has retained his strong beliefs in how drivers should drive: "Don't hold up traffic," and "If you can't drive, stay home." Sharing these maxims is something he's never shy about. He remembers a drive with his good friend legendary Portland and Multnomah Athletic Club athlete and trainer Joe Loprinzi. A gentle, non-aggressive person, Loprinzi was at the wheel. Edging into a busy intersection to make a left turn across traffic, he waited for a spot to ease into and waited through at least one turn of the light.

"Cars began to line up behind us," Bud recalls. Feeling he should be encouraging, he leaned over and said, 'Joe, you're holding up traffic. You've got to turn when you can.'" With Loprinzi still hesitating, Bud got more graphic, "Joe, see that guy behind us? He might get out of his car and come after us. And, you know what? I don't want to be in the car with you if he does!"

Loprinzi made the turn.

FUN-TO-DRIVE CARS COULD POSE CHALLENGES TO NEW DRIVERS.
PHOTO: STEVE FLOCK/BLAKE ANDERSON

SUNSHINE DIVISION

PORTLAND POLICE BUREAU
est. 1923

CHAPTER 14

BRINGING IN THE SUN

The Sunshine Division has been a staple of Portland's social service community since 1923 when poverty, homelessness and unemployment were significant challenges throughout the city. Hoping to reduce a possibly resulting crime wave, prominent Portlanders worked with the police to provide food baskets and other assistance to families in need. Their efforts grew into a unique offshoot of the Police Bureau and continue to be an important resource and a positive connection between the police and the community.

From 1963 to 1973, Bud served as commander of the Sunshine Division – a post that immediately captured his heart. His placement came after a four-month hiatus from the Police Bureau in the spring of 1963 while he attended the U.S. Army Command and General Staff College in Fort Leavenworth, Kansas. Expecting to return to the Safety Education unit where he had been director or to street patrol work, he was surprised when chief of police, the commander and the board chairman of the Sunshine Division asked him to lead the charitable program. They needed someone of high integrity, level-headedness, dignity and charm. And that someone, they decided, was Bud Lewis.

With the title of commander, Bud took the Sunshine Division to new levels of accountability both for the police bureau and those it served. He solidified relationships with the police, grocers, meatpackers, trucking firms and other donors who provided food and supplies, and worked in cooperation with community members to serve families in need. He also created a space, separate from the warehouse area, where clients could "shop" for food, clothing, furniture and other donated items.

For his staff, Bud selected people who viewed the clients the Sunshine Division served with respect and dignity. "He set the bar high," says Rob Aichele whose father was part of the division. "Being respectful and representing the Police Bureau with dignity were important. Everyone enjoyed working for him."

"He's a wonderful man," says renowned Oregonian Gerry Frank, who was on the Sunshine Division board of directors before, during and after Bud's tenure. "Everyone loved him."

TRUSTEES

The Division's "trustees" also enjoyed working with him. They were the occasional helpers – folks serving jail time for low-level crimes or maybe just living on the streets – whom patrolmen knew to be helpful and dependable. Trustees would work at the Sunshine Division during the day assisting with the sorting, packing and delivery to clients and then return to the jail at night. Sometimes 20 or more a day were in to help. "We really needed them," Bud says. "There was a lot to do." For their work, trustees could get their jail time reduced, a safe place to dry out if necessary, hot meals, and a new set of clothes. Their involvement also made them a part of a community of people who helped the larger community in need. "A few of those folks intentionally had themselves arrested so they could come in and give us a hand at the holidays. And we were grateful to have them, especially those who had muscle and could help with the heavy lifting."

A favorite trustee was Herb. "A fine person, always a gentleman, and strong," Bud remembers. "He, another officer, and I were the only ones who could pick up those sides of beef the meatpackers or grocery stores donated. We always looked forward to his help." Herb's occasional yet reliable service to the division ended after several years when he was found dead in a park. "It was a real shame, he was a good man." That's what Bud told Herb's cousin in California, the only living relation anyone could find after his death. "Even though his life was not a total success, Herb was a fine man," Bud says. "He had a lot of class and helped many, many people. I wanted his cousin to know that."

"Even though his life was not a total success,
Herb was a fine man. He had a lot of class
and helped many, many people.
I wanted his cousin to know that."

Another hard-working trustee once let on that his sister was coming to town and he didn't want her to know he was in jail. "So, we helped him out with a decent suit and a few dollars," Bud recalls. "He looked like a million bucks! She stayed in a motel while she was here and never found out he was in jail."

Bud genuinely enjoyed his time with the Sunshine Division and had great affection for the thousands of people he served there. After retiring, he has continued as a board member and is still there every year, good weather and bad, to help pack holiday boxes. In 2016, he and more than 400 volunteers packed and delivered 3,500 boxes, each with donated fresh and canned vegetables, mashed potatoes, stuffing, gravy, bread, macaroni and cheese, juice, a frozen turkey, a pie, and coupons for eggs.

Bud is also the celebrity ride-along in the police vehicle that tows the Sunshine Division's float in Portland's Rose Festival Starlight Parade. "We hear shouts of 'Bud!' all along the parade route," says Matt Tobey, the division's liaison officer with the police bureau. "He's a living legend, and an important part of our history."

Sunshine Division programs offer food and clothing assistance six days a week at their North Portland warehouse. Emergency food boxes are also available at all police precincts and through emergency delivery.

PHOTO: SUNSHINE DIVISION

COHORTS AT THE SUNSHINE DIVISION'S ANNUAL HOLIDAY FOOD BOX PACKING PARTY.

To assist or donate to the Sunshine Division, go to www.sunshinedivision.org. Tell them Bud sent you.

"*There's something special about Bud and you know it the second you meet him. There is a twinkle in his eyes, a huge smile on his face and he welcomes you with a strong handshake and a warm hug.*"

DAN BAGGETT

"*He has inner peace. He's lived a life of many eras, some not always easy, but he makes it look that way.*"

ANGELA EKELOF

CHAPTER 15

TALKING TO
THE PEOPLE

T he 1970s began with union uprisings at factories and manufacturing plants throughout the country. Labor and management
were in conflict over numerous issues. OSHA, the Occupational
Safety and Health Administration established in 1971, inaugurat-
ed new attention to workplace activities particularly in the manufacturing realm and union workers were challenging their con-
tracts and their employers. Strikes were common and sometimes
things got ugly.

In late summer of '73, ESCO Corporation's director of
security was ready to retire. A Portland-based manufacturer of
engineered products and metal components, ESCO had, and
continues to have, a world-wide reach for industrial applications.
Considering the times and thinking ahead to what might come
next for the company, the security director recommended his replacement have law enforcement experience. Six sergeants who
were about to retire from the Portland Police Bureau were considered. Bud Lewis was one of them, and Bud Lewis was selected.
Given the timing, his jump was from a softly simmering frying
pan into a smoldering fire.

A small retirement party at the Sunshine Division celebrated Bud's 31-year career with the Police Department. A Letter to the Editor in *The Oregonian* heralded his "dignity and kindness, and the friendship and encouragement he offered those he served."

In October, after hanging up his police uniform and taking a trip with Janet to Australia to visit friends made during the war (unlike his wartime cruises across the Pacific, this trip was a mere 15-hour flight), he was ready for a new adventure, this time in civilian management garb: a suit and tie.

At the time, ESCO had more than 1000 employees, most of them members of the United Foundry and Warehouse Employee's Union. Bud started in doing what anyone who knows him would expect – he met and made friends with everyone at the company. "I met every foreman, shop steward and rank-and-file employee in each of the four Portland plants," Bud recalls. With each meeting, he carried a specific message. "I wanted them to know I was part of management and that's where my loyalty had to be. But as a former police officer with a union background, I understood their situation and had concern for each of them."

"Bud had great rapport with the workers," says Randy Norris, a manager at ESCO during those years. "He had a pulse on what they were doing and wanted, possibly even more than some of the plant managers."

In January of 1974, contract negotiations with ESCO workers began. Key disputes were cost-of-living wage increases and various benefit issues. Aware that a strike might be brewing, Bud kept communication open with the union members. Based on his military and police training and knowledge of what could happen during a strike, he made sure a key message got out: Don't destroy anything that pays your wages. "I didn't want them to do anything that would prevent them from being able to come back and do their jobs," he says. "If they wanted change, I told them they should bargain for it."

The vote to strike came March 1, 1974. It passed, beginning the first strike in ESCO's 60-year history. The strike lasted 18 days, with only minor problems and plant disruption. "I spent a lot of that time at the front gate where I could watch everything and everyone who came and left," Bud says. A camera on the top of the building assisted him with that task. "I really think the fact the company had a history of treating the employees well helped a lot during that time. ESCO was always employee-oriented and the workers respected the corporation."

Bud spent nine years at ESCO before retiring. An incident that lingers with him regarded a disgruntled employee who had not received a position he thought he deserved. In retaliation, the employee damaged the casting when the metal was liquid, thus destroying the shape of the hardened mold. "We knew something was going wrong on the line, so I had a camera put up to see what was happening. And when I saw this fellow sabotaging the pour, I was really disappointed. I asked him why he hadn't talked to me. I liked him. He was the nicest guy. He just had pent up anger and that's all he could think to do."

Norris remembers being head of the United Way campaign at ESCO while Bud was there. Norris' charge was to raise funds. Bud's advice, he says, was "Talk to the people." In his years with ESCO, that's precisely what Bud did.

OFFICERS OF THE 364TH CIVIL AFFAIRS BRIGADE, 1974-75.

CHAPTER 16

Re-Upping

Military service for Bud did not end with WWII. He invested 30 more years in the Army Reserves. Those years began in 1948 when the call went out for men who met three specific criteria: they had to be 28 years of age or younger, members of police bureaus, and non-commissioned officers. Fitting the bill perfectly, Bud re-upped. He received a direct commission to the 311th Military Police battalion and soon became captain of the headquarters company in Portland. When the unit was disbanded in 1963, he joined the 364th Civil Affairs Brigade. He rose to commander after several years and, with three full-time staff members, oversaw some 100 reserve officers training for potential postings in Southeast Asia.

"Our role was to help local governments ease any impact if military operations were to come to their communities," he says. Members of his unit were called to service in Cambodia, Thailand, South Korea and elsewhere.

For his own preparation, he attended military college programs that enhanced his skills, increased his understanding of foreign cultures, and enabled him to train and command the reservists in his unit. All this was while working full time with the Portland Police Bureau and eventually with ESCO, teaching students to drive, tending to wrestlers on Friday nights, and being a family man with a wife and two children. "I was busier than a one-armed paper-hanger those years," he says, humorously remembering the active times. Flexibility at work and home was what enabled such an active lifestyle. "And I did everything I could to be a good dad," he says.

In 1975, with a total of 36 years in the military, Bud retired as a Colonel.

"When he's around, the whole world opens. He always wants people to be engaged with others."

Nan Ramirez

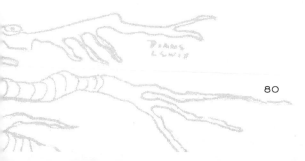

HAD ENOUGH
DOWN-TO-EARTH
COUNTRY MEETINGS?

We at the Portland Hilton know that we can't offer all the "amenities" of the country.

But one thing is for sure, when you meet at our place you can always count on certain undisputed services.

Country-fresh hot rolls and coffee to start the day's work. Microphones that don't squawk. Fourteen versatile function rooms for groups of 10 to 450 plus. (Or a grand ballroom large enough for herds of 1,600.)

And some of the friendliest meeting planners in the world.

So next time you're planning a meeting or convention, call our Director of Sales, (503) 226-7047.

We'll give you good ol' country hospitality right here in the heart of the city.

COME INTO THE **DOWNTOWN** HILTON. THE ONLY WAY TO MEET IN PORTLAND.

THE
PORTLAND
HILTON

FOR RESERVATIONS CALL 226-1611

The only way to meet in Portland, Oregon.

PHOTO: THE PORTLAND HILTON

BUD'S FIRST AND ONLY MODELING JOB. THE HILTON HOTEL DECIDED HE LOOKED LIKE THE IDEAL CORPORATE LEADER.

Rowing to victory in the MAC decathlon, 1989.

CHAPTER 17

PUNTING 61 YARDS!

A decathlon is a series of track and field and sport events that has roots in the Olympic competitions of ancient Greece. It was designed to test participants' all-around athletic skills and abilities. In the Olympic games of today, the title of World's Greatest Athlete is bestowed on the person who scores the highest points.

Every spring, Portland's Multnomah Athletic Club (MAC) holds a decathlon competition with numerous conditioning, strength and fitness events including rowing, swimming, running, sit-ups, push-ups, pull-ups, leg-press, bench-press, basketball free-throw, football punt, shot put, baseball throw, and bicycling. Ten of the events must be completed for scoring over three weeks' time. Competitors are divided into age groups beginning with the 18-to-24-year-olds and concluding with those age 65 and over. Winners are designated in each group, and the overall winner is the one with the most points. Each year, the competition attracts some 100 members.

In 1989, with 1000 total points, the most that could be awarded at that time, Bud Lewis won the MAC decathlon. He was 69 years old.

That was the first year Bud took his age group and, along with only one other member, scored higher than competitors in every age group. He scored as high again the next year at age 70, and at 71, and 72, and 73, and 74. In '91 and '93 he was the only competitor to be the overall winner.

For six years straight Bud amassed 1000 points. At age 74, he decided it was time to retire. Although he admits there are times when it's best to transition from one pursuit to another, his departure from the decathlon was not because he felt, in any way, old.

His best times and efforts, some of which continue to be MAC records, include:

- Push-ups – 120
- Pull-ups – 30
- Football punt – 61 yards
- Baseball throw – 272 feet
- Basketball free throws – 31 (out of 35 attempts)
- Leg-press – 900 lbs.
- Bicycling –100 pts (as much as allowed)
- Bench-press – 245 lbs.
- Rowing – 2500 meters in 10 min. 7 sec.
  (putting him at 12th in the world for his age group)
- 100-yard dash –13.9 seconds
- Sit ups – 85/minute

Still standing after all these years are Bud's scores for football punting, basketball free throws, and sit-ups.

Indeed, those '89 through '94 wins were milestones. They claimed broad attention – from those who appreciated athletic achievement and from those who might have thought age meant reduced ability. "I saw Bud make that record-breaking 61-yard football punt," says Pete Greer, past MAC Assistant Athletic Director, who was in his 30s at the time. "It was incredible! Most of the rest of us were kicking 30 to 40 yards and here comes this guy in his 70s and he just booms it! It was inspirational!" "He beat all the studs and young guys coming out of college!" adds competitor Sandy Koski.

As to whether age was a factor in his desire and intent to do well, Bud does not let on. He admits that his accomplishments required effort, as they would for anyone at any age. It took 11 years for him to hit that 1000-point mark. His first year in the competition was just a year after he joined the Multnomah Club. In 1978, with 903 points he won in the 55-to-59 age group and was second in the overall competition. For the next few years, he came in just shy of the 1000 mark.

From the beginning, time and strength were on his side. While still employed full time, he carved out daily noontime runs followed with strength-training exercises. He alternated muscle groups so as not to cause undue strain. Being strong, he had muscles that were already developed so he focused on enhancing ability and stamina. After retiring, he expanded the routine although he was careful not to push harder than necessary. "There's a burn-out factor," he says, "I enjoyed the challenge but I wanted to have fun with it."

HELPING OTHERS SUCCEED

Involvement in the decathlon allowed Bud to do what he does best: encourage, inspire, and promote. In 1978, he was designated as one of the MAC's "Co-Competitors of the Year." Two years later, the MAC decathlon committee established the Bud Lewis Outstanding Competitor award to "honor participants who have similar qualities to Bud, including a strong sense of competition and a willingness to help others succeed."

"He was always there encouraging and cheering people on," remembers 1980 MAC decathlon participant Candy Puterbaugh. "He'd ask how you were doing and offer advice." He also actively encouraged others to participate. "He would stand outside the weight room recruiting people to go into the decathlon," recalls Darrell Duvauchelle, MAC's Fitness Manager. "He'd say 'Well, you're a big strapping fellow. You should be in the decathlon.' And he's always so positive. He just loves to see people being active."

And he continues to persevere. In May of 2017, at age 96, 22 years after his last decathlon, Bud decided he wasn't done. He entered the MAC's decathlon to compete again. "I wanted to test myself to see if I could do it," he says. His 10 events, completed in two-days (considered the Iron Man category), were the 1000-meter row, bench press, 40-yard shuttle run, shot put, football punt, 100-yard dash, basketball free throw, stationary bike, 100-meter swim, and the 200-meter swim. "And I found I could do it," he says with an infectious smile. A smile that invites others to keep trying, too.

Since 1988, the Multnomah Athletic Club has bestowed the Joe Loprinzi Inspirational Award on a member who emulates the spirit, enthusiasm and ongoing interest in fitness Loprinzi set forth as an example to all. Bud Lewis was the first recipient of the award.

AT AGE 96, AGAIN IN COMPETITION

*"He's inspiring and
legendary."*

HOWARD HEDINGER

PHOTO: SANDY KOSKI

BEAUTIFUL STURGEON HOOKED ON THE WILLAMETTE RIVER.

CHAPTER 18
LOOK AT THAT!

Nature warrants appreciation. Offering it is one of Bud's great and constant gifts. Whether a bird, a flower, or a sunset he notices and invites others to join him. Ask his deer hunting companions about the time he stopped them in their tracks with a gasping "Oh my goodness!" Anticipating a nearby herd with perhaps an 8-point buck at the lead, they reined their horses and raised their rifles, trigger fingers at the ready.

"Look at that flower!" Bud exclaimed. "Isn't that beautiful?!"

"He'd see some flowers or sumac and get more excited than anyone looking for a deer," says Jay Olson, whom Bud has joined on many trips to the wilderness. "He just loves watching for whatever is out there. He enjoys looking for deer but he never reaches for his gun. It's the experience and being in the moment with nature that's important."

Shooting an animal is something Bud can be relied on not to do. Though he sees nothing wrong with anyone else doing it. If someone gets a deer, he's quick to help with the field dressing, skinning, and hauling of the carcass back to camp. And he's in line for the grilling, basting, and eating, especially if there's plenty of accompanying garlic and onions.

Sport shooting, however, something he has done in the past, is no longer necessary. "I just don't want to take a life," he says. "We're all nature's animals, and I really feel I have no right to shoot another one. I guess the older I have gotten the more respect for life I've gained."

All it took was one shot. Bullseye.

"I caught him looking through the scope of his rifle once and thought this would be the year he'd actually take a shot," Olson says. "But it turned out he'd forgotten his binoculars and the only way he could see a deer in the distance was through the scope!"

Not that he couldn't get the shot if he had the desire. When Bud was into his 70s, his hunting companions surmised that perhaps those military/police marksmanship skills might be a bit rusty. They tempted him with a four-inch target 200 yards away. "OK," he said.

All it took was one shot. Bullseye.

Fishing is another story. Bud will reel them in as long as they're biting. And no catch and release frivolity. Catch and fry is his great pleasure. Fellow fisherman Sandy Koski tells of fishing with Bud and another angler when Bud was in his late 80s. They caught 36 sturgeon in four hours with Bud getting his fair share. "He got a bit tired after the first six, so we rigged up a harness so he could sit. And he kept catching!"

On another trip, Pete Greer tells of Bud catching something, no one was sure what, and working at bringing it in for nearly a half hour. "It turned out to be a big old carp," Greer says. "Most people think of carp as junk fish, but Bud looks at it and says, 'Look at the beautiful scales on it!' And we're saying, 'It's a carp!' and he says, 'But it's so beautiful!'"

Not shooting animals but hooking fish? "That is a puzzle," Bud admits. "I guess I'm shaped by my culture. The reality is fish are going to die soon anyway. They swim upstream, do it, and die. That's sad! The female digs a hole and the male fertilizes the eggs. And that's all it is. They don't even get to kiss!"

Indeed, animals-versus-fish poses an anomaly, but an allowable one when the enjoyment of nature, friends, and beauty is at its roots. "Being able to see beauty widens your whole horizon," he says. "We have enough sorrow in this world – we need something to buoy us. That's what nature can do. It's power and beauty combined."

That combination, Bud believes, is most evident at Oregon's Crater Lake. "Tremendous power blew Mount Mazama off the face of the earth and it created such magnificence. That lake is as blue as can be. Few places have that power and beauty together. When I go, I think I'd like to be there – as stardust on the brink of the lake with my Janet."

"THE BEST THING IN THE WORLD"

WHAT'S THE BEST THING IN THE WORLD?
JUNE-ROSE, BY MAY-DEW IMPEARLED;
SWEET SOUTH-WIND, THAT MEANS NO RAIN;
TRUTH, NOT CRUEL TO A FRIEND;
PLEASURE, NOT IN HASTE TO END;
BEAUTY, NOT SELF-DECKED AND CURLED
TILL ITS PRIDE IS OVER-PLAIN;
LOVE, WHEN, SO, YOU'RE LOVED AGAIN.
WHAT'S THE BEST THING IN THE WORLD?
--SOMETHING OUT OF IT, I THINK.

BY ELIZABETH BARRETT BROWNING, 1855

Bud Lewis

BLOOD DRIVE

The May annual blood drive is now named in honor of MAC member Bud Lewis, who has been a faithful supporter of members donating blood for decades.

MAC
WELLNESS

Stop by, shake Bud's hand and sign up for a timeslot!

CHAPTER 19

GOING FOR BLOOD

"If they could see you, they'd line up for your blood."

Who wouldn't give blood after an enticement like that? It's one of Bud's lines to lure people into the Multnomah Athletic Club's twice yearly blood drives for the American Red Cross. With clever come-ons, he energetically supports both events, particularly the Bud Lewis Blood Drive held in May that commemorates his more than 20 years of very active participation.

Although his WWII bout with hepatitis prevents him from giving blood, it's a cause he strongly supports. "There's nothing more profound a person can do than give of their life to someone else," he says. "Even Bill Gates can't do more than that."

"He's saved hundreds of lives," says Keri Donovan, MAC Wellness Coordinator. "Bud is an important part of our blood drives and of getting people to donate. Plus, he knows everyone! They come up to the table to talk with him and he ropes them in to signing up."

According to the Red Cross some 38 percent of the U.S. population is eligible to donate blood at any given time. Fewer than 10 percent, however, actually donates. Each of the MAC's drives attracts some 80 donors and provides the Red Cross with nearly 120 pints of blood. A single donation may help up to three people.

MAC member Greg Marshall who has worked the donation table with Bud during the drives says members rush up to the table and give him a hug. "People gravitate to Bud like moths to a flame. And he's happy to see them all," Marshall says. "He seems to know everyone's name. And if he doesn't he's good at not letting on."

Donor Recruitment Representative for the Red Cross, Elizabeth Butler, says the MAC blood drives are important to their overall donation program. "If Bud's not there, we know it! We're very grateful for all his support."

Juice and cookies are always rewards for donors at any donation site. At the MAC, donors also get a handshake from Bud and some special words, "The person who's getting your blood can't thank you, but I'm thanking you for them."

To donate blood, contact any Red Cross Donation Center, www.redcrossblood.org, or call 1-800-REDCROSS. (Bud thanks you.)

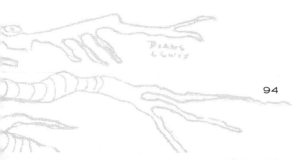

*"What Bud models is
something anyone can do.
But not everyone puts their
energy and time into it."*

PETE GREER

*"Bud makes everyone happier and
better by simply being around."*

KEVIN KELLY

BUD WITH MEMBERS OF
LINCOLN HIGH SCHOOL'S 2014 WATER POLO TEAM.

Chapter 20
Cheering Them On

On Saturday, Nov. 14, 2015, Bud arose at 4:30 a.m., got into his car and drove 84 miles to Corvallis where Lincoln High School's water polo team had a match against Lakeridge High School in the state water polo finals. As the team mascot, Bud needed to be there to cheer them on.

Bud has gone to nearly every match Lincoln's water polo team (boys and girls) has been in for the past 10 years. He's been to most of their practices, too. "He's a team icon," says Tyler Sinner, coach for the 2015-16 year. Kyle Corbett, team captain for that year, says he's considered the "Team Grandpa."

And it all began because he could hear them.

When Bud first met the team, they held their practices in the pool at the Multnomah Athletic Club alongside the lane where he swims laps. Hard of hearing for many years, he appreciates it when voices are loud enough for him to hear without his hearing aids, and Billy Martin, the coach at the time, had what Bud describes as "a voice like a fog horn." That gave little opportunity not to know what was going on. It was also obvious the kids were working hard, and having fun. So of course, he paid attention.

Each day after his laps, Bud chatted with the players, asked about their strategies, commented on their technique, and cheered them on. "Come to a match," Martin urged one day. So of course he went, and to the next one, and the ones after that. He got to know the coach, the players, the parents. And they got to know him. At season's end, he arranged and paid for a pizza party that has become an annual event.

"I've met some of the nicest kids," Bud says. "I've watched them grow. Those kids are fantastic athletes. Water polo is one of the toughest sports there is. You could drown if you didn't pay attention!"

"He talks with us, asks how we're doing and gives us encouragement. He's a constant supporter," Corbett says. Indeed, with the team having numerous coaches since Martin and members who move on, Bud has been the mainstay over the years.

"I've met some of the nicest kids. I've watched them grow."

"From day one as a new coach I knew Bud had a huge impact on the team," says Sinner. "Parents and players were always reminding me about the 90-year-old man who comes to every game - home or away. They described him as Lincoln's number one fan." Before and after each game, Sinner says, kids would go up to him to chat. "His words of encouragement have been a huge help to young athletes who can be easily discouraged when times are difficult."

Sinner even credits Bud with helping hold the team together during years when wins eluded them. "Without Bud," Sinner says, "I think the team would have lost members out of discouragement. It would have been difficult to form a team at all, let alone a competitive one."

Recognizing the value of his encouragement, the team has created the Bud Lewis Award. It is bestowed on a team member who "has the qualities we've seen in Bud," Sinner says. More specifically, it's for a player who "gives the extra effort, communicates with the team, wants to learn, asks the questions on how to improve, and wants to get better each day."

Past coach Tori Buck raves about Bud's involvement with the team. "He is so genuine and cares about our success. He brags to everyone about our awesome program. He is a special man."

"Bud's an inspiration and full of life," Corbett says.

"He always has great comments for everyone," says parent Rosaline Elfick. "I hope I'm partying with teenagers when I'm in my 90s!"

"The connection Bud has with kids is remarkable. They look at him and admire him for his spunkiness, his love for life. "

NORM RICH

THE MAN AND HIS CAR.

Chapter 21

Enjoying the Drive

Bud's first car was a 1926 Model T Ford. He paid $10 for it and an additional 50 cents to register it. He bought it from the neighbors despite knowing his mother would not let him keep it. He couldn't afford the gas, she would say, he couldn't get insurance, she would say, there was no place to park it, she would say.

It was 1936, Bud was 16 years old and owning a car seemed the most marvelous thing in the world. So, for however long he could keep it, he wanted that car. It was black, as were all Model Ts. (As Henry Ford so famously put it, "Any customer can have a car painted any color he wants so long as it is black.") Bud's had a magneto ignition system and had to be cranked to start. "You could break your arm if you didn't crank it just right," he remembers. It could go up to 45 miles an hour (although he "never" drove it faster than 25). All his friends wanted a ride – in the car or on the running boards.

And he loved it. For the two weeks he had it.

His mother, of course, found out about the car and stated the reasons he couldn't keep it: he couldn't afford the gas, he couldn't get insurance, there was no place to park it. So he relented and sold it to a friend. Figuring his two weeks of use depreciated the car somewhat, his selling price was a dollar less than he paid for it. "Can't make money when you think like that," he now says. Nevertheless, it was a prophetic purchase. Ford's Model T was ultimately named the Most Influential Car of the 20th century, 16.5 million were made and it opened automobile travel to more Americans than any other car. More importantly, it put Bud on the road to being a "car guy."

Years later, after marrying Janet, and their two children came along, the first Lewis Family Car was a two-tone green 1948 four-door Nash Custom 600. Made by the Nash Kelvinator Corporation of Kenosha, Wisconsin, it was the first mass-produced American automobile constructed with a consolidated body and frame. It was quieter, lighter and more rigid than other cars, and it could go 600 miles on a single tank of gas, providing the driver did not drive faster than 30 miles an hour. "We paid $1,572 cash for it and thought it was wonderful," he says.

Ford's Model T was ultimately named the Most Influential Car of the 20th century, 16.5 million were made and it opened automobile travel to more Americans than any other car.

Through the years many cars have followed, including a 1966 Nash Ambassador Club Coupe that had a black exterior, gold interior, and a big engine. "It was beautiful, one of the nicest cars I've had," Bud says. Until, of course, his current one – a 2016 Nissan Maxima Sports Sedan - the Platinum Model, pearl white exterior, ebony black leather interior. Nimble, sporty, exceedingly "fun to drive." It replaced his old car – a 2013 Nissan Maxima Sports Sedan. The 2013 had only 21,000 miles on it when he took it in for maintenance, spied the newer model and was taken by its beauty. "I drove it and thought, oh man, I like it!" The next day, it was his.

Most likely, he admits, the 2016 will be his last car. "I really have no business buying a new car. But this is an elegant sports car. I just decided I'm going out with flair."

He and a friend have plans to take it out to a race track. "I'm going to see if I can get it up to 120!"

"Bud Lewis makes me
want to be a better everything –
man, father, friend,
son, husband, brother."

DARIN VICK

"CBS SUNDAY MORNING," MAY 29, 2016.

CHAPTER 22

HELPING END HATE

Perhaps it's the weight of the reality of his WWII service: "Directly and indirectly I handled every round of ammunition 3,333 soldiers used against the Japanese for two years." Perhaps that's what makes being able to forgive important to Bud. "I helped create havoc for the Japanese and participated in the wounding and killing."

So many years later, he now sees a different world, enemies who once fought to the death are strong friends and allies. With that, he believes, comes the need to honor and acknowledge both sides. "You can't hate forever," he has said. Those words have given him national, even international recognition.

In March of 2015, when KOIN 6 News of Portland wanted to do a story on WWII, they looked to Bud as one of the veterans who could help present the topic. The story centered on the humanitarian non-profit OBON Society, based in Astoria, and its efforts to bring reconciliation and closure between the nations through the act of returning WWII mementos to Japanese families. "OBON" is a Japanese word that refers to remembering and respecting ancestors.

The specific items the OBON Society is assisting with are Yosegaki Hinomaru or Good Luck Flags, tokens of home that Japanese servicemen took with them to war. The flags were white silk with the red sun of Japan in the middle. Surrounding the sun were messages family and friends added wishing the soldier power, victory, safety and luck, and reminding him to do his duty for his country - possibly an acknowledgement that it was not expected the warrior would return from battle. The interpretation of Yosegaki Hinomaru is "writing together around the Japanese flag."

The flags often became souvenirs of war for U.S. servicemen encountering dead Japanese soldiers on the battlefields.

KOIN's story attracted the attention of CBS News and the son of a U.S. serviceman who felt the need to return the Yosegaki Hinomaru he found among his recently deceased father's things. Having been in the same division as that deceased serviceman, Bud was again sought to help tell the story. "I provided the ammunition that killed many of those folks," he told the CBS producer. "And I'm not totally happy I did that, but at the time that was my job. I couldn't question it." The story then followed the U.S. serviceman's son to Japan to meet the son and daughter of the Japanese soldier and to give them their father's flag.

By Summer 2017, the OBON Society had returned 120 Yosegaki Hinomaru to Japanese families, with more flags coming in all the time.

"It's closure," Bud told the CBS producer, "You can't hate forever."

For more information about the OBON Society and their humanitarian work, go to www.obonsociety.org

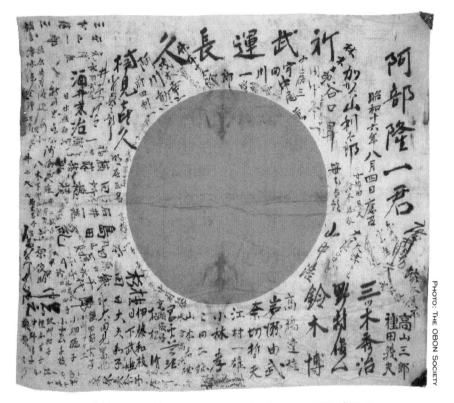

A Yosegaki Hinomaru awaiting its return to Japan.

PHOTO: THE OBON SOCIETY

THESE 10 MEMBERS OF THE OREGON NATIONAL GUARD SERVED TOGETHER IN AUSTRALIA AND NEW GUINEA AND AGAIN AS PORTLAND POLICE OFFICERS. BUD IS FRONT ROW, LEFT.

CHAPTER 23

CHERISHING GOLDEN FRIENDS

From early on the soldiers of the 41st Division got together for annual reunions. They started in 1948 when the men were still young and undoubtedly still awed at where they had been, what they had seen, and what they had done "over there," oblivious to the idea that merely doing their jobs made them part of the "greatest generation."

As the years passed, the get-togethers offered times to re-fight battles, laugh at the conditions they endured, debate the strategies that they, the foot soldiers, were sent to carry out, and mourn those they left behind. "Memorabilia time," Bud calls the reunions. "It's time to get together with brothers and talk about things others wouldn't understand. You would have died for these people, and they would have died for you."

Reunion trips to Australia have taken place at various times over the years, too. In 1992, a half century after they had first arrived in Australia 14,000 soldiers strong, some 30 members of the 41st Division returned together - thrilled to find that memories of them had not faded. In Townsville, Queensland, they marched in a parade feted by cheering, flag-waving Aussies who remembered, or had learned, what these aging Yanks had done to protect their country. "Lots of people were in the streets," Bud remembers. "It was a huge event. People came up to us and shook our hands and kissed us!"

Other events have recognized the soldiers over the years, abroad and at home. In 2009, a new, nearly 250,000 square foot training and operations facility at Camp Withycombe in Clackamas was dedicated to the 41st Infantry Division and its soldiers' WWII service. It was named the 41st Infantry Division Armed Forces Reserve Center and is the largest Oregon National Guard facility. Speaking at the groundbreaking ceremony were Major General Raymond F. Rees, then the adjutant general of the Oregon National Guard, and Ted Kulongoski, then governor of Oregon. Representing the WWII soldiers of the 41st was Bud Lewis who received a standing ovation and was described on OregonLive as a "beloved elder."

Rees, whose posting with the Oregon Guard began in 1987, remembers reaching out to Bud in his desire to recognize the history of the 41st Division and its WWII legacy. "Bud was the wheel horse – the one who carried the load in gathering everyone. Every time there was an opportunity to bring the people of that era together with the more modern era, Bud was there to do it. He was always helping, and never thinking about himself. He's always thinking about other people."

Dave Funk, Rees's staff assistant who coordinated that 1992 trip to Australia, worked with Bud to help design the historic remembrances on display in the new training facility. The collection contains more than 14,500 artifacts. "It's been a real joy to be involved with Bud over the years," Funk says. "He's such a positive guy. He has a memory like an elephant and a tremendous command of history."

Bud was also a key interviewee in a video documentary about the 41st Division that is taken to schools to help students understand WWII history. "The Jungleers," conceived of and directed by Lt. Col. Alisha Hamel, offers narratives and detailed descriptions of the soldiers as they made their way through New Guinea in pursuit of Japanese strongholds. "Bud was my 'go-to' guy in helping tell the story," Hamel says. "His memory is amazing. And he doesn't brag about anything he did over there. He just wants to make sure the 41st Infantry is not forgotten."

When they went to Australia in 1942, the 41st's 186th Regiment Service Company, the one that had Bud driving trucks and passing out ammunition, had 160 members. In 2017, one remains. "I'm the last one," Bud says. "It's a good feeling because I'm alive. But I'm sad because I'm the one who can't talk to a whole host of wonderful guys I knew a long, long time ago."

"WITH RUE MY HEART IS LADEN"

WITH RUE MY HEART IS LADEN
FOR GOLDEN FRIENDS I HAD,
FOR MANY A ROSE-LIPT MAIDEN
AND MANY A LIGHTFOOT LAD.

BY BROOKS TOO BROAD FOR LEAPING
THE LIGHTFOOT BOYS ARE LAID;
THE ROSE-LIPT GIRLS ARE SLEEPING
IN FIELDS WHERE ROSES FADE.

BY A.E. HOUSMAN (1896)

A VISIT FROM BUD LEWIS IS A HIGHLIGHT AT
MANY COFFEE SHOPS AROUND TOWN.

CHAPTER 24

LIVING A DAY

Unless he's heading off on a rafting/camping trip with friends, Bud's day might start with breakfast at one of the many restaurants where the workers look forward to seeing him. "We love him," says Julie O'Kelly who works the counter at the uptown Zupan's Cafe Umbria. "He's like our store mascot. I've never known anyone who is as kind to everyone as he is. One day there was a fellow here who might have had some mental issues, and Bud walked up to him and said 'Hi, I'm Bud Lewis, how are you?'"

A meeting to discuss the Sunshine Division, a blood drive or an upcoming athletic event could follow breakfast. And then he might have lunch at another of his favorite haunts perhaps the Cider Mill in Southwest Portland. "He's a true gentleman," says Mercedes who often greets and serves him there. "For everything he's seen, and he's seen the good and the bad, he still has a great outlook on people and on life. I think he's an awesome person."

After returning home, he might sit on his deck to watch and commune with the birds who know that seed is always available. Such communing, however, is not always peaceful. "I've been in a battle with a squirrel," he admits with more than a little vehemence. "Squirrels have to live, too, but I don't want to feed the squirrels, I want to feed the birds." Bud's initial plan of attack was to bang on the window to scare the squirrel away. "But I didn't want to break the window, and it didn't work anyway. That squirrel just sits right there, eats the bird seed and defies me!"

Later in the afternoon, after Bud and the squirrel come to a truce or one gives up, could be a workout at the MAC – 30 minutes of lifting weights and 30 minutes of swimming laps.

Following a shower might be a stop at one of the club's dining areas either for an ice tea and a bowl of popcorn or a dinner of razor clams, liver and onions or possibly a prime rib sandwich. "I met him when I started working here. He asked me where I'm from," remembers Carlos Quezada, a MAC dining employee and a native of Lima, Peru. "He was so excited about my being from Peru. We talk whenever he comes in. He asks how I am and how my family is. He has a big heart."

"He may come in alone," says Laura Gulinello, a MAC restaurant manager, "but he doesn't stay alone. People gravitate toward him. There always seems to be a crowd around him."

The magnetism of Bud Lewis is obvious as he makes his way through many public spaces. When out to dinner with him one evening, his daughter Diane and a friend wagered over the number of people who would come over to chat while they ate. "We stopped counting at 35," she remembers.

Indeed, people seek him out. They even seek him in. While in the hospital in the Spring of 2015 receiving a bovine valve to repair a damaged aortic valve ("I asked for an angus bull valve, but they said they didn't have that technology yet," Bud jokes) he was nearly swamped with visitors. "A nurse asked me if he was a celebrity," says Cookie Tohl who works in the MAC's Mporium boutique and had stopped at the hospital to say hello. "She said it was unusual for a person his age to have such a steady flow of people coming to visit. She also said they were really enjoying having him there."

He wasn't in the hospital long and was soon back to his routine of meeting friends, exercising and engaging, in some manner, with the birds and the squirrel.

At 97, Bud keeps looking for new opportunities. "There are things I haven't done that I want to do," he says. "And I'm not getting any younger so I'd better get going." Next up? "Well, I haven't tried skydiving...."

"THE RUBAIYAT OF OMAR KHAYYAM"

AWAKE! FOR MORNING IN THE BOWL OF NIGHT
HAS FLUNG THE STONE THAT PUTS THE STARS TO FLIGHT:
AND LO! THE HUNTER OF THE EAST HAS CAUGHT
THE SULTAN'S TURRET IN A NOOSE OF LIGHT.
DREAMING WHEN DAWN'S LEFT HAND WAS IN THE SKY
I HEARD A VOICE WITHIN THE TAVERN CRY,
"AWAKE, MY LITTLE ONES, AND FILL THE CUP
BEFORE LIFE'S LIQUOR IN ITS CUP BE DRY."

AND, AS THE COCK CREW, THOSE WHO STOOD BEFORE
THE TAVERN SHOUTED—"OPEN THEN THE DOOR!
YOU KNOW HOW LITTLE WHILE WE HAVE TO STAY,
AND, ONCE DEPARTED, MAY RETURN NO MORE."

FIRST TRANSLATION BY
EDWARD FITZGERALD, 1858
QUATRAIN 1, 2, 3

*"His dedication to wanting to
learn and know more,
both about topics and
people, is infectious.
His genuine smile makes
you want to start a conversation
with him, and his wit makes
you want to continue it."*

ELLEN BARON

CHAPTER 25

BEING AWARE

Cars, blood drives, athletic endeavors, friends young and old, falling shoes, natives with spears, and the beauty of flowers and fish - topics Bud enjoys. His conversational repertoire, however, does not stop there. It easily ventures toward eastern and western civilizations (current and ancient), religions of the world, evolution, literature, physics, philosophy, geography, archeology or a book he's reading. Those who cannot keep up best settle in for an intellectually invigorating, if humbling, ride.

"I might cause people to think," he says a bit mischievously. "It's important to be aware."

Among his favorite topics is the role of religion throughout the ages, one he approaches both with fascination and some irreverence. "I'm not going to get a seat at the right hand of God," he admits. "But, it's probably crowded there, anyway." Too bad. His presence would surely add to the discourse.

Another significant theme for him is the transience of time. Omar Khayyam's eloquent expression, "The Moving Finger writes and having writ, Moves on..."* is a favorite of his, as is scientist and educator Stephen Jay Gould's pragmatic concept that the hu-

* "The Rubaiyat of Omar Khayyam" First translation by Edward FitzGerald, 1858, Quatrain 51

man species is occupying only "the last inch of the cosmic mile."* "We're here for a short time," Bud acknowledges. "We should not think too highly of ourselves."

Sages he looks to for inspiration and doses of reality include Neil deGrasse Tyson, Richard Dawkins, Galileo, and 11th century Persian philosopher and physician Avicenna. Those with curiosity, skepticism, intellect, and lack of complete adherence to preconceived or prevailing beliefs resonate with him.

Ben Johnson, William Shakespeare, Alfred Lord Tennyson and other classical poets attract him for their simplicity and elegance in telling stories and interpreting ideas. Twelfth century conqueror Genghis Khan interests him for the egalitarian view of allowing people to think and worship as they wished.

---

*"We're here for a short time.
We should not think too highly of ourselves."*

He admires people who take risks to stand for issues they believe in despite potentially dire consequences. Examples include celebrated Olympic and professional boxer Mohammed Ali who spoke out against the Vietnam War resulting in a suspension of his boxing career, and Oregon Senator Wayne Morse, one of only two U.S. senators who opposed allowing the president to take military action in Vietnam without a declaration of war. Morse's stance ultimately cost him his senate seat. "Both Ali and Morse stood up to tell the truth," Bud says. "That takes courage."

Nearer home, for many years Bud looked to close friend and kindred spirit Joe Loprinzi (1914 - 2009) for deep conversation

*"I Have Landed" Stephen Jay Gould, 2002

and contemplation. "Joe and I were great friends. He was so wise and he really cared about people. I appreciated his thoughts and his belief in the value of both physical and mental activity. I especially agreed with his very wary view of success. He believed the best measure of success is how one achieves it and reminded us all not to equate money with success. He was a great thinker, a great motivator and a wonderful friend."

"I believe in the four Ds:
dedication, determination,
desire, discipline.
If you feel good physically,
you feel good mentally."

JOE LOPRINZI

BUD WITH HONOREES OF THE FIRST
MULTNOMAH ATHLETIC FOUNDATION'S BUD AWARD.

CHAPTER 26
SHARING OPPORTUNITY

Bud credits the Multnomah Athletic Club for offering opportunity to him and others. His many years of involvement have brought him nearly every award given to senior members and recognition of him has earned him the informal designation of "mayor and ambassador of the MAC."

In his honor, the Multnomah Athletic Foundation has developed the Bud Award, a community grant presented to non-profit organizations that exemplify sportsmanship, enthusiasm, and a passion for athletics. Based on Bud's desire, highest priority recipients are those that provide access and opportunities to youth from underserved communities. The 2017 award was given to the athletic program at De La Salle North Catholic High School in Portland. In presenting the award, Bud celebrated with De LaSalle students Traveon Johnson, Elsy Herrera, and James Broadous, Dean of Students/Athletic Director.

To contribute to the Bud Award or gain more information, go to www.multnomahathleticfoundation.com

"Prospice"

Fear death? — to feel the fog in my throat,
　　The mist in my face,
When the snows begin, and the blasts denote
　　I am nearing the place,
The power of the night, the press of the storm,
　　The post of the foe;
Where he stands, the Arch Fear in a visible form,
　　Yet the strong man must go:
For the journey is done and the summit attained,
　　And the barriers fall,
Though a battle's to fight ere the guerdon be gained,
　　The reward of it all.
I was ever a fighter, so—one fight more,
　　The best and the last!
I would hate that death bandaged my eyes and forbore,
　　And bade me creep past.
No! let me taste the whole of it, fare like my peers
　　The heroes of old,
Bear the brunt, in a minute pay glad life's arrears
　　Of pain, darkness and cold.
For sudden the worse turns the best to the brave,
　　The black minute's at end,
And the elements' rage, the fiend-voices that rave,
　　Shall dwindle, shall blend,
Shall change, shall become first a peace out of pain,
　　Then a light, then thy breast,
O thou soul of my soul! I shall clasp thee again,
　　And with God be the rest!

By Robert Browning, 1861

CHAPTER 27

KEEPING THAT STRONG GRIP

Having been born with the umbilical cord wrapped around his neck, losing a tooth to high school football, persevering through malaria and hepatitis, cancer of the esophagus, a serious bacterial infection of the spine, aortic valve disease, and the passing of his beloved Janet, how did Bud get this far? And what keeps his grip so strong? His optimism, energy, clean living, and deep appreciation of an ageless, friend-filled life certainly have helped. Though he's known to offer an occasional "It's hell to get old," anyone hearing it might well wonder just when "old" might arrive for him, and to hope it remains a long way off.

As to how he's made it this far, surpassing many of his contemporaries, Bud says he doesn't really know. "I think it's a combination of things. It could be genes and habits. My mom and dad lived to older age, and I'm kind of an old stick-in-the-mud about what I do." He confesses to being a teetotaler, although he does admit to an occasional gin and tonic ("One is medicinal, two is just drinking"), to a mai tai ("If I'm in Hawaii"), and to that one beer back in '63. "I remember it well. Drank it while standing on my head."

That beer was part of a ceremonial rite while he was at a gathering of military police at the U.S. Army Command and

General Staff College in Fort Leavenworth, Kansas. "Think of it, standing on your head with your feet on the wall and drinking a beer! I don't like beer and it didn't help that I was standing on my head! But that's the only one I've ever had."

Tobacco is something else Bud has stayed away from. "My dad told me if I wanted to play athletics smoking would interfere with my endurance, so I decided not to start." Such decisions, he believes, can determine lifespan. "People who smoke and drink a lot are making decisions that could shorten their lives. Yet, if they want to have a blast before they go, there's nothing wrong with those decisions. They're just not ones I've made."

And then there's attitude.

Physical fitness has held life-long importance to him. It has taken him from his school years through the military and the decathlon years and on to his current swimming and weight-lifting regimes that have allowed his return to the decathlon. The benefits have been clear. At 97, his grip remains strong.

And then there's attitude. "I'm always pretty high. I'm never low. I've never had any depression. I've had baggage, but I think I've overcome it." What about people who don't have that outlook and opt for the low instead of the high? "Some people like clouds better than sunshine, so that's what they see," he says. "I like sunshine, so that's what I see. Clouds are necessary, but I don't want to see them all the time."

Which leads to his signature trait, the one anyone who knows Bud can rely on. "I cheer people. I'm good at encouraging. I say come on, come on, you're not done. I believe people can do more than what they think, especially when someone helps them along."

Maybe it is a combination of all of the above, with a little luck thrown in. "I'm the luckiest guy in the world," he firmly believes. "I've had great opportunities, done lots and lots of things, and I've met tens of thousands of people whom I enjoy and keep enjoying. Much of it has seemed like throwing a rock in a pond. I never know where or how far the ripples from that rock are going to go."

Strong grip, ripples that keep going, roots that spread.

*"I believe people can do
more than what they think,
especially when someone
helps them along."*

BUD LEWIS

126

Legend has it
if you stand near a
Giant Sequoia
you can feel its
energy.

BIBLIOGRAPHY

Browning, Elizabeth Barrett. "The Best Thing in the World." *The Complete Poetical Works of Elizabeth Barrett Browning,* Cutchogue, New York: Buccaneer Books, 1993.

Browning, Robert. "Prospice." *A Treasury of Great Poems English and American,* edited by Louis Untermeyer, New York: Simon and Schuster, 1942

Burns, Robert. "A Red, Red Rose." *The Complete Poetical Works of Robert Burns.* Student's Cambridge Edition. Boston, Massachusetts: Houghton, Mifflin and Co., 1897

Fitzgerald, Edward. *The Rubaiyat of Omar Khayyam,* First Translation. Quatrain 1, 2, 3. Garden City, New York: Dolphin Books/Doubleday & Company, Inc., 1970.

Gilman, LaSelle. *The Golden Horde.* New York: Smith and Durrell, Inc. 1942

Gould, Stephen Jay. *I Have Landed.* (A collection of essays from *Natural History Magazine.*) New York: Penguin Random House, 2002.

Housman, A.E. "With Rue My Heart is Laden." From the collection, "A Shropshire Lad." *A Treasury of Great Poems English and American,* edited by Louis Untermeyer, New York: Simon and Schuster, 1942

Shelley, Percy Bysshe. "Ozymandias." *The Norton Anthology of English Literature.* New York: W.W. Norton & Company, Inc., 1968.

Acknowledgments

Many fascinating, lively discussions with Bud and interviews with many wonderful people who are part of his world have brought about this book. Viewing life through Bud's wise, all-seeing and always positive eyes is an endless pleasure. Hopefully, these stories extend that opportunity to readers.

This book is compact, and intentionally so. The idea of doing more with less has always attracted Bud, and so the stories and events of his first 97 years are presented in a way that honors that attraction. Much more, of course, could be said!

My thanks in the preparation of this book goes to those many friends of Bud's who spoke with me of their experiences with him. Specifically, I want to thank the folks at the Sunshine Division, the Portland Police Museum, the Oregon Military Museum, the Multnomah Athletic Club, the OBON Society, the Hoyt Arboretum and the Lincoln High School water polo team. I am also indebted to David Funk, Alisha Hamel and Warren Aney for their WWII knowledge, to Jan Jackson for her skillful and tactful editing skills, to Diane Lewis for her artistic skills, to Sherry Wachter for her great design skills, to my family and friends for their encouragement, and to Bud Lewis for being a continuing inspiration to us all.

36737251R00078

Made in the USA
San Bernardino, CA
27 May 2019